loveladies

**Creative appliqué**

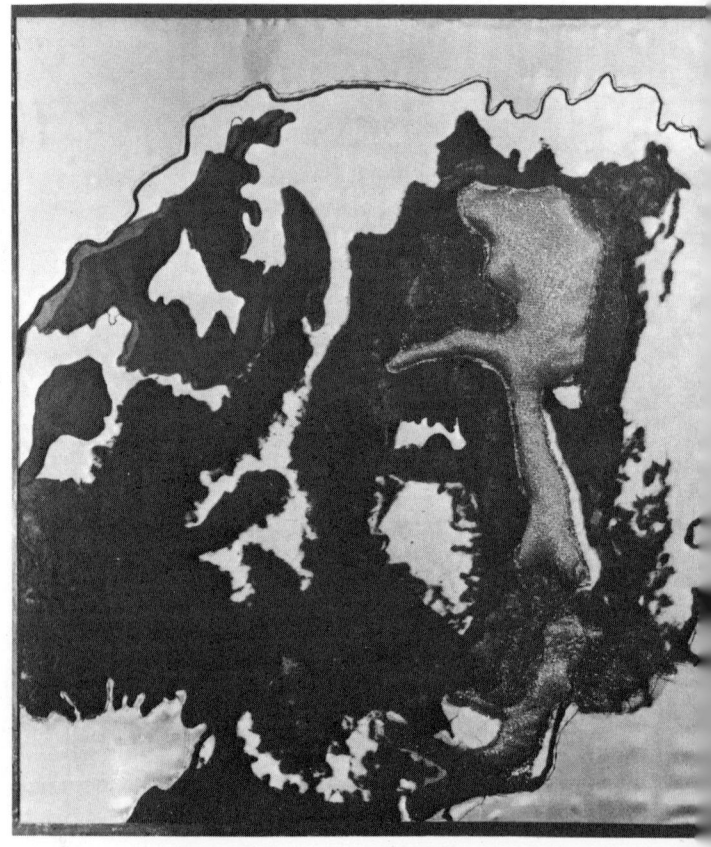

*Shadows* by Dorothy Moore. Appliqué, using net, satin, linen, Lurex and fleecy domette. Tones of red with black

# Creative appliqué

## Beryl Dean

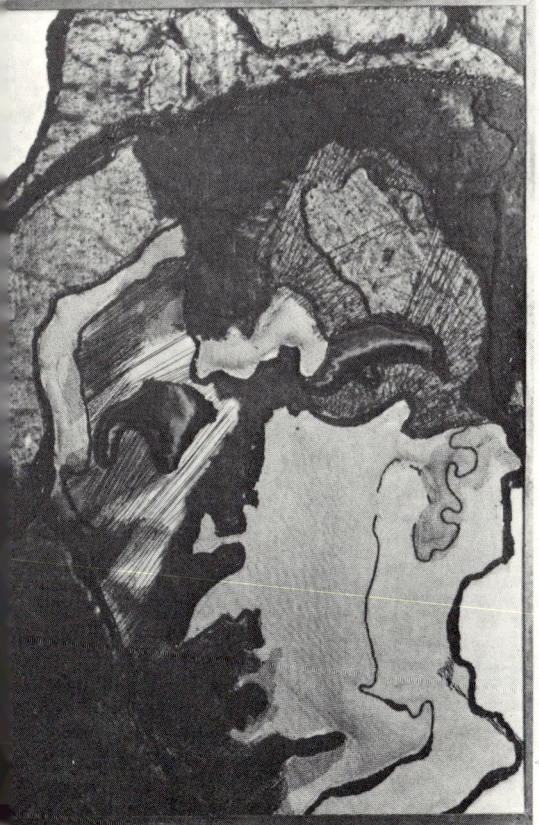

**Studio Vista London**
**Watson-Guptill Publications New York**

## Acknowledgements
The author would like to thank all the artists whose work appears in this book, and also the following for allowing their photographs to be reproduced: Joan and Thomas Simmons, figs 3, 4, 10, 11, 29, 37, 51, 52, 62, 67, 68, 69, 73, 75, 77, 85; Mason Bryar Studios, figs 16, 49, 66, 74, 96 and frontispiece; W. S. King, figs 30, 78; Peter Balestrero, figs 38, 50, 53; J. E. Lawe, fig. 58; Ian Ross, fig. 64; Anthony Burrett, fig. 65; Jack C. Adams, figs 79, 88; the Smithsonian Institution, Washington, D.C., fig. 93.

Figs 5, 6, 71, 72, 89, 90, 94 and 95 are reproduced by permission of the Victoria and Albert Museum, London, and fig. 92 is reproduced by permission of the City of Birmingham Museum and Art Gallery.

General editors Janey O'Riordan and Brenda Herbert
© Beryl Dean 1970
Published in London by Studio Vista Limited
Blue Star House, Highgate Hill, London N19
and in New York by Watson-Guptill Publications
165 West 46th Street, New York 10036
Watson-Guptill ISBN 0-8230-6575-8
Library of Congress Catalog Card Number 73-118011
Set in 9 on 9½pt Univers
Printed and bound in Great Britain by
Bookprint Limited, Crawley, Sussex
UK SBN 289.79708.X

# Contents

|    | Introduction 6 |
|----|---|
| 1  | Designing for appliqué 7 |
| 2  | Fabrics 16 |
| 3  | Equipment and the use of embroidery frames 23 |
| 4  | Transferring the design 28 |
| 5  | Creating in appliqué 32 |
|    | Methods and types 32 |
| 6  | Further techniques 54 |
|    | Surface stitchery in relation to appliqué 54 |
|    | Appliqué in limited colours—practical uses 57 |
|    | Lettering in appliqué 64 |
|    | Padding 66 |
|    | Expressing yourself 66 |
| 7  | Decoration as part of construction—practical uses 70 |
| 8  | Machine embroidered and stitched appliqué 74 |
| 9  | Appliqué for the church and theatre 81 |
| 10 | Finishing and mounting 89 |
| 11 | Historical background 94 |
|    | Further reading 103 |
|    | Index 104 |

# Introduction

The revival of interest in appliqué as an embroidery method during this century is the outcome of circumstances characteristic of the times – the desire for speed, the lively interest in the constantly changing new fabrics, and the emphasis on spontaneous creativeness in all forms of art. For the inexperienced, and for children, appliqué will provide a means of self-expression and an almost instantaneous way of communicating ideas with fabrics, scissors and simple stitchery, and they will discover immense pleasure in moving cut-out shapes around and experimenting without any very clear objective; while the more experienced artist with a serious approach to a carefully considered composition will find its realization in terms of appliqué just as exciting.

Another reason for the popularity of appliqué is its scope and adaptability. A wide range of ideas can be developed, from the small detail to large-scale projects, and from the purely decorative to the utilitarian, all of which are both rewarding and stimulating.

Unlike collage, which is pasted or glued together, appliqué is composed of fabrics held down and enriched with stitchery. Most embroidery techniques demand some specialized knowledge and practice, whereas, if you have the desire to create with fabrics, the simplest form of appliqué can be started quite spontaneously without previous experience. All you need is a piece of fabric for the background, odd bits and scraps of fabric, scissors, needles, pins and threads, and off you can go! The magical quality of fabrics will spark off unpremeditated ideas; these can grow and develop spontaneously in a satisfying way, which will make you want to get going without being held up by tiresome or boring preparation. This is fine. Let nothing stop or interrupt the flow and drive of inspiration; go ahead, capture the idea in terms of appliqué, and do not be put off by lack of experience. From these beginnings, progressively more ambitious projects can be undertaken and experience will help you decide which of the methods outlined in this book you will want to use.

It cannot be overstressed that the whole purpose of the book will have failed if it leaves you with the impression that good results cannot be achieved without following all the technical advice suggested. But as you progress, you will find that learning about the more precise practical methods will make further development of your work possible and will help you to achieve better and more durable results, without in any way lessening the enjoyment experienced when undertaking free appliqué.

At the end of the book you will find a necessarily brief historical survey which may further stimulate your interest.

# 1 Designing for appliqué

It is possible to emphasize this particular facet of design, but to treat it in complete isolation would not help beginners. An understanding within a wider context is more constructive. Some people have a natural sense of design, whereas in others it can be developed; these, at the start, seem to find that with a conscious formula they gain confidence.

Certain basic tenets are common to all design. First must come the idea. This may be derived purely from the imagination or may be stimulated by observation. That inner 'seeing eye' explores and visualizes pattern and decorative possibilities in everyday things, such as chimneys, leafless trees, church spires against the sky, waves, pebbles, rocks, shells, kitchen utensils, wood graining and tree bark, marble, vehicles, wheels, buildings, plant forms, feathers, animals, fur, etc.; the list can be endless. Make a practice of recording these impressions by sketching, and so storing them up for future use. These drawings bear the imprint of personal interpretation, and later the forms can be simplified and adapted to create a design (figs 1 and 2).

Fig 1  Peter Brown lives on a farm, observes and sketches the animals he knows so well

Fig 2  *Cows* by Peter Brown based on the sketch in fig. 1, with the characteristics preserved and decorative qualities developed

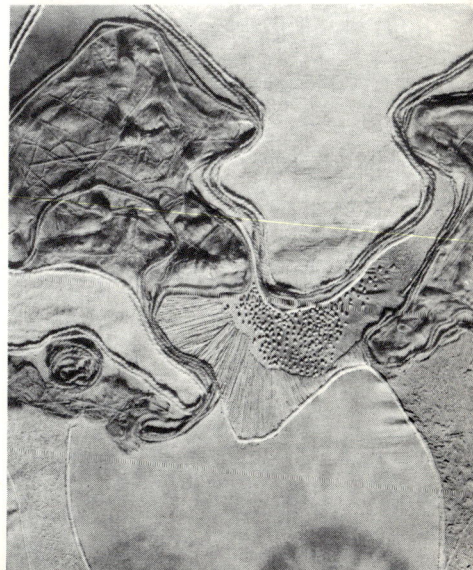

Fig 3  A page of pressed leaves, taken from a scrap book

Scrap books are also invaluable as sources of inspiration. They can contain a fragment cut or torn from a photograph, some accidental find, perhaps some impression of a brass rubbing or a small part of a reproduction of a painting, skeleton leaves, etc. (figs 3 and 4). At first you will choose obvious things such as drawings of teapots or plants from seed catalogues; then by degrees your selection will become more ambitious and, for example, the pattern value of an enlarged photograph of an eye will be included. Later you will recognize the design possibilities

Fig 4 Showing how the leaf forms in fig. 3 could be developed into a pattern by using cut papers, etc. When enlarged this design is suitable for appliqué in nets, lace, organdie, etc.

to be derived from turning it vertically, and cutting it in half. In this way an original approach is established, which replaces the choice of hackneyed, often-repeated, subjects.

Secondly, after choosing the subject – perhaps, for instance, an aerial photograph of a fly-over (over-pass) – how do you set about making the design? It may help to cut a window from a piece of paper and move this frame around until the part of the photograph which will make the best design has been found. Then decide which of the roads form a composition of rhythmical lines, also consider whether the shapes between the lines are good. This is specially important when the idea is to be realized in appliqué, as these are the shapes which will be blocked in as 'mass'. The next stage may be to cover the whole with tracing paper and draw in, very freely, the lines of the roads, eliminating those which are unnecessary to the whole, and making other adjustments which might be an improvement, paying attention to the background shapes. Instead of enlarging this in the usual way, the result has an added quality when blown-up photographically.

A design can be contrived in several ways. Another method is to make an arrangement with torn, cut or 'found' paper shapes of different kinds and textures, paying special attention to their interest and variety; though they should not be too varied or too unrelated. By using some transparent and overlapping shapes, other unexpected results may emerge. The design can then be developed with the addition of superimposed lines. As with all design, it is the distribution of 'mass' upon the background which is important. An equal amount of pattern to background is boring, as this represents the proportion of half and half, whereas a third to two thirds is more satisfactory. A grouping of all the shapes to one side, leaving only background on the other, may cause unsatisfactory imbalance, though this can be rectified by moving over some of the smaller shapes and so making an interesting composition which is balanced without being symmetrical. This method of designing for appliqué can be carried out spontaneously by using fabrics, cords, etc., which can be pinned to the background. This has the advantage of being seen vertically, and from a distance, which makes visual judgement and correction possible throughout.

It is not often that the embroidery method pre-determines the type of design; much more usually the design comes first, then the choice of technique for its realization follows. However, you might have some special reason, such as finding scraps of exciting textures, for wanting to do appliqué, so the character of the design subject and the colour scheme would then grow out of the particular pieces of material. It might be abstract or geometrical or an arrangement of repeating shapes; alternatively, a formalized figure could be suggested (figs 5 and 6). Probably the best way to set about doing a design would be with a large brush, charcoal, wax chalks, or ink, using thick paints and watercolour on rough paper with very free, strong strokes contrasting with the areas of texture, so that tension is set up which will make the design come alive.

To set out to design for a particular type of embroidery (in this instance, appliqué) does narrow down both the subject matter and the approach to the preparation of the design. Another method is to cut out, very freely, various permutations of the design motif,

Fig 5  One example of a formalized figure. Burmese Court Lady, mid nineteenth century. Silks pasted to a thin backing, then cut and applied to black wool cloth. Light pinks, greens and cream, with superimposed linear designs in silver cords and sequins. Victoria and Albert Museum

Fig 6  Burmese Kalanga, nineteenth century. Green, cream and black wool and cotton applied to a red wool ground. A balanced arrangement of formalized figures, architectural and plant forms. Victoria and Albert Museum

conventionalizing it and making it decorative, also concentrating on the main form rather than details which can be added afterwards. For this, you might well use collage for your design, with all sorts of materials, papers, string and odds and ends glued to textured paper. The most satisfactory variation could then be translated into appliqué.

To allow the construction of the object to determine the decoration may spark off many ideas which can be carried out in appliqué; for example, in dress ornamentation, handbags and bags of all kinds, cushions, curtains, bedspreads, household linen and church vestments. In common with all designing, good spacing

and attention to proportion is important; so, too, is the fitness for purpose. This practical application will be dealt with later in the book.

To recapitulate – the salient points to be borne in mind when designing for appliqué are:

1, to plan in terms of mass, concentrating upon good large shapes;
2, to realize that the areas of background are of equal importance;
3, generally to keep the interest towards the middle, but not in the centre;
4, where applicable, to form a rhythm within the composition;
5, to watch the scale of the design;
6, to see that the spacing is interesting and balanced and that the proportions are varied and well planned as a part of the whole.

I would suggest that you study the illustrations in relation to these points, seeking reasons where there are exceptions.

## Colour

Both as a personal experience, and as a means of expressing emotional perception, colour is of fundamental importance. One's reaction to and use of colour is, to a great extent, instinctive: this is an advantage which outweighs a knowledge of colour theory. However, some generalizations may help in certain circumstances.

There are three primary colours–red, blue and yellow. The secondary colours (orange, green, purple) are produced by mixing two primaries, and the tertiary colours are formed by mixing a primary with a secondary. A hue is one colour as distinct from another.

An awareness of tone is important in colour. This is the relative darkness or brightness of the hue, depending upon the amount of black or white mixed with it. Neutral colours can be warm (these usually have some of the reddish colours mixed with them), or cool (with a blueish tint).

The appreciation of tone extends the use of colour. A scheme composed mainly of, for example, red with yellow-orange and dark purple at full strength will vibrate in its brilliance, but it will not possess the subtlety of a scheme composed of greenish and yellowish greys with black or white.

By using contrasting tones, the dynamic factor is introduced: but this is not only a matter of placing dark and light in opposition, it is also the juxtaposition of warm and cold hues, the use of complementary colours, the proportion and shape of the areas of colour, and the degrees to which pure and diluted colours are used; to this may be added the areas of texture.

So much depends upon the intuitive deployment of colour, even the shape of the area matters; according to its positioning a small patch of colour can possess an intensity equal to that of a large area, and discord, unacceptable at one time, gives pleasure and vitality.

An appreciation of colour can be developed further by taking natural objects and really observing them, as if seeing them for the first time. Look at a pile of broken stones after rain, a passion flower, or the plumage of a pigeon, for example. Then set yourself a series of experiments in relation to appliqué, by finding fabrics which suggest, first, the colours, and second, the textures in all these objects.

Other studies might be made using materials to illustrate contrast of tone, in greys chromatic and achromatic; tones of one hue; several colours; contrasted areas, shapes and proportion of colour. Endless pleasure can be derived from exploring the

Fig 7 *Sun in the trees* by Audrey Walker. A variety of silks, nets, metallic fabrics, and velvet ribbons are applied on a pale cream coarsely woven furnishing (upholstery) fabric. Ribbons are also threaded through long straight stitches. Additional texture is provided by French knots. Colours are mostly muted greens, gold and cream

variants of one colour, then extending the visual impressions resulting from personal observation.

There are associations connected with certain colours; red with heat, blue with cold, etc. There is secular symbolism. But above all, there is liturgical symbolism (cream, white, gold, red, green, purple and rose-pink), its usage developed from the early days of Christianity. All these can be taken into account when designing a colour scheme.

## 2  Fabrics

One of the great advantages of appliqué is that there need be no expenditure, as most people either have a bit (scrap) bag, or can get hold of odd pieces of fabric. All embroiderers are avid collectors of scraps, indeed they develop both acquisitive and miserly tendencies towards materials.

There are certain methods of appliqué where the whole surface is covered with applied shapes, and therefore only a backing material need be used, such as linen, unbleached calico, etc.

However, it is more usual for parts of the background to remain exposed, therefore its aesthetic properties are important. For example, if a dull, matt surface is envisaged, then moss crepe, fine dress-weight wool or a man-made fibre mixture would be suitable, and if a little bright shine would contrast in an interesting way, duchess satin, wild silk, dupions (slubbed fabric), silks from Thailand, many other interesting weaves for dress and furnishing (upholstery) fabrics can be used.

For large-scale undertakings, where a texture is required for the background, coarse hand-woven linens, silks and mixtures are interesting; so too is raw silk, there are lovely ones of Indian origin. There are also all sorts of unexpected fabrics such as hessian (burlap) etc.

There are now more fabrics on the market than there have ever been and because of the excitement engendered by their variety appliqué continues to be very popular.

When considering what makes for a good background, it is important to remember that it must be firm and not too thick. It is in any case always advisable to mount the background material over a backing, which may be linen, unbleached calico, holland, almost anything that will add a little 'body'; this is an added precaution against puckering.

It is almost impossible to give precise suggestions for the choice of materials suitable for appliqué if it is necessary to purchase some for a particular purpose, because new synthetic and man-made fibre weaves and mixtures are constantly introduced or withdrawn, and the importation of others discontinued.

However, there are basic factors which determine the choice of fabric: the first is that it will not fray; the second, that it will not stretch out of shape; and the third, that it will lie flat and, above all, will not pucker. Also, it should not be too bulky. Some of these faults, if they are encountered, can be overcome to a great extent by applying iron-on Vilene (Pellon) or Stayflex, etc., to the back. These are obtainable in several thicknesses, but cannot be used on very thin materials. Their introduction has almost entirely

Fig 8 *Apex* by Anna Yelland. Various fabrics, including copper, tarletan and velvet, in brilliant colours

Fig 9 *Waterfall* by Audrey Walker. Applied suede, nets and silk on a cotton furnishing (upholstery) fabric, with pearls, beads, mirror glass, and a variety of threads – mostly couched, but also French knots and straight stitches

Fig 10  *City at sunset* by Kay Chapman, Mary Boon Comprehensive School, London. A variety of fabrics in purples, greys and flame colours, with surface stitchery
Nursery hanging by Diane Poole, Mary Boon Secondary School, London. Appliqué in red, dark blue, white and yellow felts

superseded the use of pasting and starch-soaked muslin for appliqué.

The easiest material to manipulate is coloured felt; more interesting is very fine jersey knit, and fine dress weight wools or PVC. You need to be constantly observant, and collect short lengths of exciting things whilst they are available. Contrasting textures can be introduced by using velvet, needlecord, kid, suede and the type of material known as suedette, brushed nylon, even dish cloths and curtain net. And many dress and furnishing fabrics can be used.

The one fundamental trouble that must be avoided, because the remedy is so difficult, is puckering. The inexperienced embroiderer is courting disaster if she combines very thick wools with very thin fragile fabrics. With this exception, most fabrics can be used if care is taken with the preparation.

Very typical of appliqué today are the elusive translucent effects obtained by using transparent materials; organza, nylon, crystal nylon, chiffon, net and gauze are all used single or with several thicknesses. Broken and merging colours can be contrived; this becomes practical if one transparent layer is spread overall, and invisibly caught down at intervals. This is a useful tip, so remember to arrange first the odd small coloured pieces, they may be kept in place with tiny stitches or a very small drop of latex glue such as Copydex (Sobo in U.S.). Lastly, cover the whole with some very transparent fabric.

To turn in the edge of transparent materials often spoils the effect, though it adds strength. One way to prevent fraying is to spread a small amount of some adhesive such as Copydex or Sobo (which goes transparent when dry) a little way in from the edge, and then cut through this. Tiny stitches can be sewn over this edge. Sometimes to singe or treat the edge with heat will prevent nylon from fraying. Light or dark transparent invisible thread is useful and the stitches hardly show.

It is advisable to include some hand or machine surface stitching over parts of applied transparent materials, not only because the contrast adds charm to the design, but because it gives additional strength.

Another idea which could be developed is only possible when a transparent ground is used. Try applying areas or shapes of more strongly coloured opaque and transparent fabrics to the back. This is prepared in the same way as for ordinary appliqué, except that it is on the back and the design is reversed. Superimposed embroidery on the front adds to the interest. This is very effective when mounted between two pieces of perspex (Plexiglas) or glass, for coffee table tops, place mats or trays (fig. 58).

The scale of the design for these delicate fabrics will obviously be smaller and more detailed than it would be for a heavy curtain, hanging, or room divider, for which the choice of material might be a heavy hand-weave from hand spun wool, with felt and kid applied. Scale, being a satisfactory balance between the size, weight, design and purpose, is most important when planning appliqué.

For present-day design inspired by Art Nouveau, smooth, closely woven fabrics give the best results, because of the intricacies of shape found in the counterchange characteristics existing between pattern and background (fig. 12). If the edges are to be turned in and hemmed, then a fine silk or cotton applied to a closely woven dress-weight tweed or flannel might be

Fig 11 Cut-out units from patterned fabrics, arranged in various permutations to form the design, then stitched to background with added embroidery

Fig 12 Shiny black PVC applied to a woollen fabric, edges invisibly sewn down with restrained addition of embroidery

suggested; but a cut edge can only be satisfactory for such a design if it has been rendered non-fraying, or, for example, felt has been used.

There is a tendency now to appreciate the juxtaposition of similar shapes, placed and cut from different directions of the fabric, so that they all change colour according to the angle at which they are viewed. Although usually carried out in collage, the same idea is suitable for appliqué.

The collection and subsequent arrangement of differently patterned fabrics can be made into most interesting compositions, which possess individual characteristics when applied to the right background (fig. 10).

Some scrap of printed or woven fabric may be the inspiration or basis for further stitched development which grows out of the design (fig. 11). Units of pattern cut from material and applied, then enriched with embroidery, which may or may not be repeated to form a larger concept, will help to solve the design problem.

We have seen how endless are the exciting ideas which can be created by applying variously textured and coloured materials, and how the contents of any scrap-bag will yield up pieces of velvet of rich colouring, thin silk, novelty rayons, sumptuous satins and silks, shot taffetas, poult, metallic yarns woven with other threads, fragments of Indian gauze, fascinating little pieces of printed silks and cottons. The illustration on the cover is an excellent example. So do allow yourself to become inspired and enjoy experimenting, even if you have never attempted any embroidery before.

# 3 Equipment and the use of embroidery frames

For appliqué you need two pairs of really sharp scissors, one pair for cutting out the fabric and another small pair of embroidery scissors with good points; a selection of needles, crewel and sharps; steel pins, sewing and embroidery threads; and tracing paper, pounce, a fine paint brush and watercolour paint for transferring your design (see page 28).

For machine stitching and embroidery, you will need one of the many electric sewing machines now on the market. Their use is discussed in chapter 8.

A large sheet of soft board is useful at the planning stage, as you can pin (tack) into it, and the background fabric can be pinned (tacked) out flat whilst the pieces to be applied are moved around before being tacked (basted) into position; and as the work proceeds it is possible to prop the whole thing up to judge the effect from a distance. A board is also useful for the process of stretching (see page 89).

Embroidery frames are often required when accuracy is necessary, and to prevent puckering. There are two kinds: the slate frame (fig. 13) which is the kind ordinarily used, and the circular tambour (drum). They can be bought or made. The length of the webbing denotes the size of a slate frame. Sometimes a picture frame will serve the purpose.

### To frame up or dress a frame

If you enjoy creating spontaneously and very freely, then the following instructions are not for you! You can go straight on to page 32. Otherwise, the information will be found useful, not only because a frame could be constructed from the drawings (figs 13 and 14), but because the use of an embroidery frame can be an invaluable aid when undertaking appliqué for a banner or hanging, etc.

The method described here refers to framing-up a backing, but when a backing is unnecessary the same method is used for the background fabric.

1  Cut the material (backing or background) at least 1 in. larger than the finished size of your work, and preferably with the selvedge grain running from top to bottom.

2  Mark the centre: then fold down $\frac{1}{2}$ in. at the top and bottom.

3  On both sides fold a $\frac{1}{2}$ in. turning over fairly fine string, then run stitch, with the odd back-stitch for added strength (fig. 13A).

4  Next, take the rollers (B) and mark the centres of the webbing on each one. Put the centre of the top edge of the backing

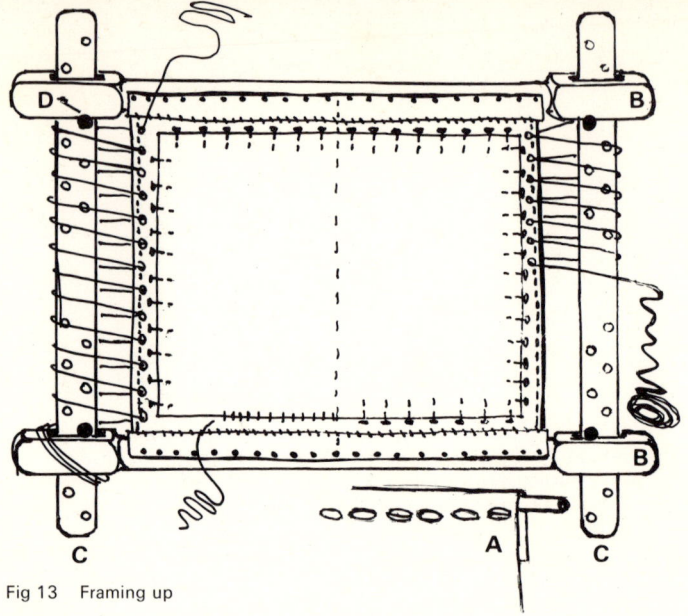

Fig 13  Framing up

material, wrong side down, to the centre of one roller: pin outwards towards the sides. Repeat for the second roller.

5   Using a strong thread (button thread is suitable), overcast the edges of the backing fabric to the webbing. Fig. 13 shows the result.

6   Slip the side pieces or slats (C) through the slots at the ends of the rollers.

In the diagram a rectangle of fabric the required finished size is shown. But when a piece is needed which is considerably longer than the side pieces, then wind the extra length round one or both of the rollers before slipping in the slats. (For additional width a bigger frame is needed.) The extra length will be released or rolled up when necessary as the work progresses.

7   Put in the four pegs, or split pins (D), checking that the distance between the rollers on each side is identical. The pegs are adjusted so that the fabric is absolutely taut for transferring or for executing the actual embroidery, but the frame is left slack when fabric is to be applied.

8   Take a length of string, sufficient to do the whole of one side without a join, and thread into a packing needle, then lace this through the backing and over the slats, as in the diagram. Either pull this up really tightly or leave it fairly loose according to your requirements. Fig. 13 shows the whole thing fairly slack, with a piece of background fabric in position upon the backing (selvedge grain to selvedge grain).

Fig 14    Mounting a large area of fabric on a smaller frame

9    Then, pulling very slightly outwards, stitch background to backing, first the top and bottom, then the sides.
10    Tighten up the frame and the lacing, and tie off the string.

## Framing up for a large area of fabric

To overcome the problem of a small design on a big expanse of background, for example, a bedspread:
1    Frame up a piece of backing (firm but thin such as calico, linen, holland or muslin) large enough to take the size of the decoration: leave slack.
2    Put the whole of the fabric upon the frame, with the appliqué design over the backing. Smooth it out and pin, keeping the pins in the same direction throughout, then zig-zag tack (baste) (fig. 14).
3    Fold up the surrounding material, then tighten up the frame. Now transfer the design if it has not been done previously (see page 28).
4    When the work has been completed, the surplus backing can be cut away.

As it is impossible to reach for more than about 15 ins when working, a long piece of backing can be framed-up and rolled round; it can be unrolled, and more of the background fabric unfolded as the appliqué is completed. For this it is convenient to have a second and longer pair of side arms or slats.

### A METHOD OF FRAMING UP FOR A VERY LARGE PROJECT

Few people need or would want really huge embroidery frames, although a quilting frame, being lighter, can sometimes be used. Apart from this obvious solution there is a simple way to tackle the problem of areas of appliqué scattered upon a large field of background.

Fig 15 *Flames beyond trees* by Elizabeth Kerr. No preparatory design was drawn for this panel. The background red and black furnishing (upholstery) fabric has a slubbed yarn with specks of colour which suggested the scheme of yellows, pinks, reds, browns and navy blue. Scraps of many-textured materials were cut and arranged directly on to the ground, and a flame-like pattern virtually evolved by itself. These lines were not transferred to the panel but freely translated by stem stitch and couching in black knitting yarns, chenille and cotton Perlita (3-ply mercerized embroidery thread with a shiny finish)

1  Frame-up permanently a piece of very firm linen, then cut away from it a rectangle, oval or circle, (the edges may be strengthened with blanket stitch for a longer life). This is in no way a backing.

2  Put the whole of the background fabric upon the frame, with the area to be worked over the hole in the framed-up linen. Pin in position, then tack (baste). Roll up the surplus fabric around the sides.

3  When this area of work has been completed, remove the tacking (basting) stitches and lift the fabric off (assuming that no stitches have been taken through to the linen by mistake). Then repeat the process, moving another piece of the design over the hole, and when it has been worked, remove it and repeat as often as necessary.

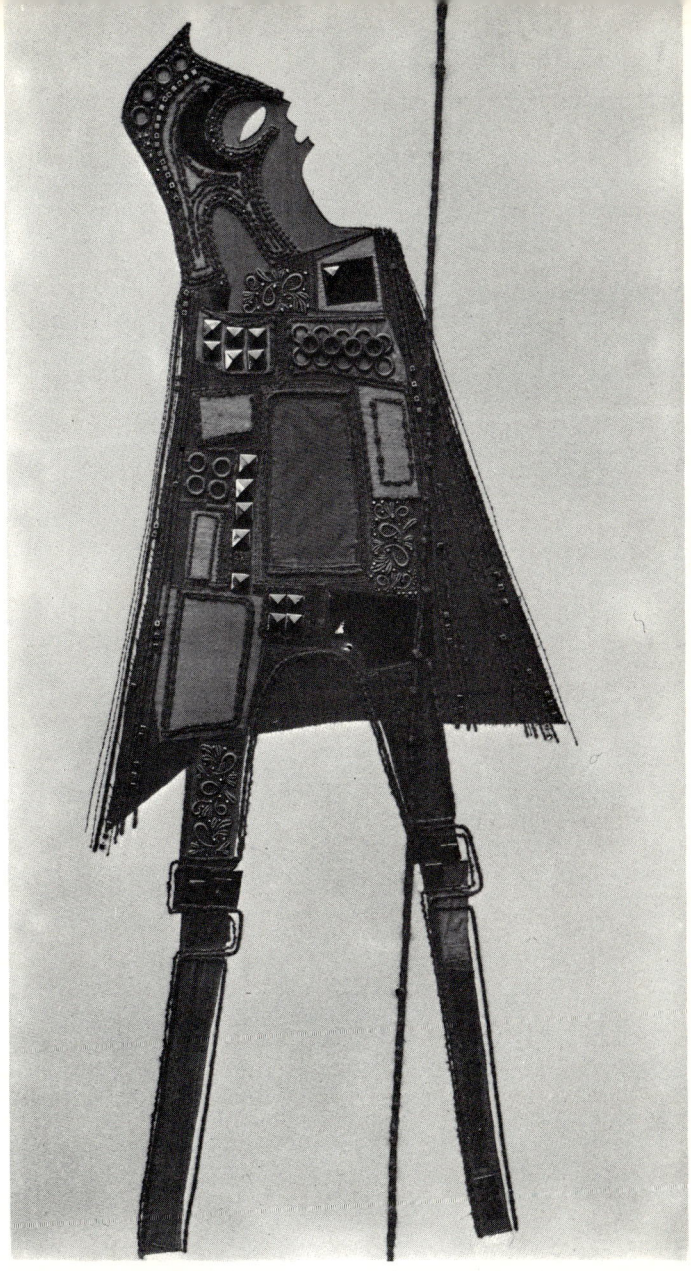

Fig 16 *Warrior* by Rosalind Floyd. To a ground of yellow ochre, fabrics of many textures have been applied, also studs, rings, etc.; though all are black they appear as different tones

# 4 Transferring the design

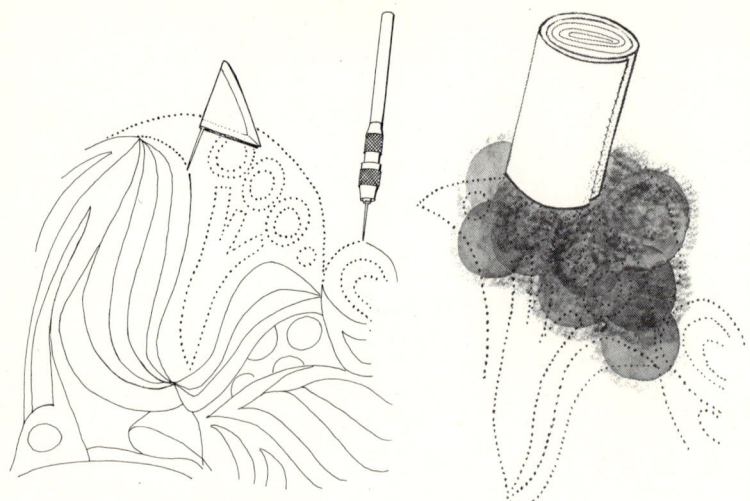

Fig 17  Perforating the tracing
Fig 18  Rubbing on the pounce

The various different techniques and ways of approaching appliqué are described step by step in chapter 5. If you are starting with a piece of free appliqué and want to work spontaneously, you will not need to mark out your design on the fabric with great accuracy. But for the more precise and conventional methods, transferring the design to the fabric is essential and has always proved something of a problem. One of the following methods will probably be found to be a solution.

*Method 1* – **Pricking and Pouncing**
Advantages – accuracy; capable of endless repetition.
1   Trace the design on tracing paper, mark the centre.
2   Fit a size 9 or 10 needle into a pin vice or small cork, or make a little holder by folding and re-folding a small square of paper into triangles (fig. 17).
3   Place the tracing over folded felt or blanket, and perforate the outlines (fig. 17).
4   Place the perforated tracing in position upon the background fabric, using small weights to prevent it shifting. The whole process can either be done with the fabric pinned out, or after it is framed up.
5   Decide whether to use black pounce (powdered charcoal) or white (powdered cuttlefish or French chalk) or a mixture of both.
6   Make a pouncer by rolling up a strip of felt.

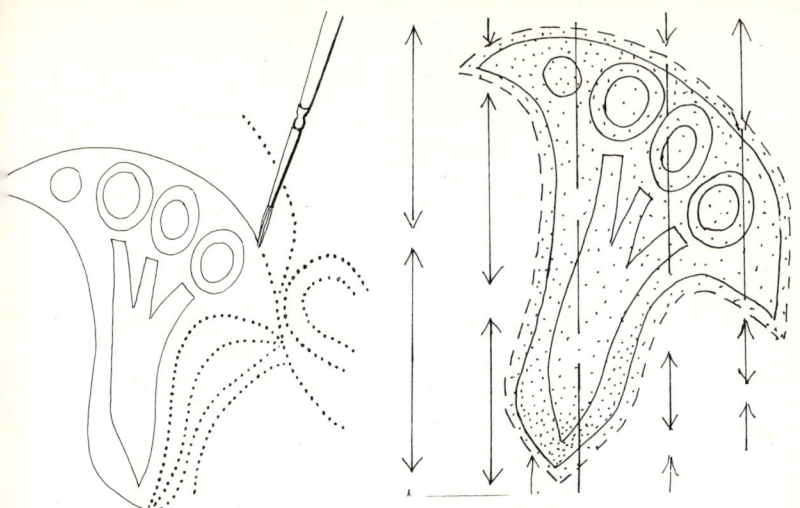

Fig 19  Painting the outline on the fabric

Fig 20  Marking the direction of the grain of the background fabric upon the shape to be applied

7   Dip the flat end into the pounce, flick off surplus, rub the pounce through the perforations, using a small circular movement (fig. 18).

8   Remove the weights, lift off the tracing, and clean it by rubbing it over with a cloth.

9   Using a fine sable brush, paint in with watercolour the lines made by the pounce on the fabric (fig. 19). Start at the corner nearest to you and cover finished parts with tissue paper. Try to complete the whole in one operation, because if left the pounce can blow away.

10   Flick off the surplus pounce with a clean cloth.

11   The outline is painted on to each of the pieces to be applied in the same way. Care must be taken to see that the grain of the material of every piece corresponds with that of the background (fig. 20) unless there is a reason for not doing so (see page 46).

Where permanent outlines would be a disadvantage, it is possible to tack (baste) them, instead of painting, if care is exercised. An experienced worker might prefer to paint or tack (baste) certain key points or lines only.

*Method 2* – For an alternative method which saves time, rub in the pounce and remove the tracing as before, then using Reeve's Fixative Spray, go over the surface of the fabric with the aerosol spray. Test the material before starting, just in case the fabric is affected in any way.

*Method 3* – Another method of transferring the design to the fabric, which has the advantage of leaving no permanent line, is to

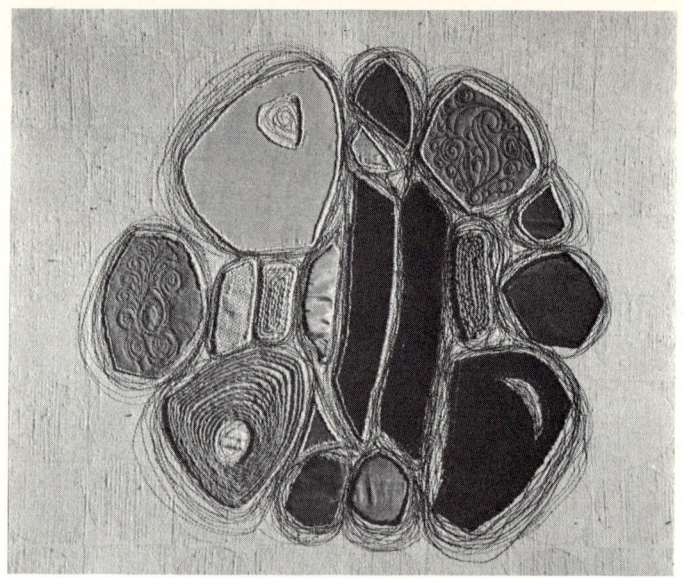

Fig 21 *Moving sun* by Elizabeth Kerr. On light orange furnishing fabric with a formal, tapestry-woven, circle motif, a freely drawn circle of yellows, oranges, pinks, rust and reds was built up with areas of stem and coral stitched knitting yarns, but mainly by applying materials of varying textures with variable satin stitch on the Irish machine (a trade machine for special techniques). These areas were blended together and into the background by spiralling lines of machine-sewn straight stitching, and additional texture was achieved by machine-stitched decoration 'drawn' on some applied areas

trace the design on to tissue paper: if you run over the lines with a dressmaker's tracing wheel, it can be torn away more easily. Tracing paper can be used, but because it is tougher, the stitches may get pulled out when it is removed.

Next, pin the tissue paper to the fabric, and tack (baste) in the lines, making back-stitches at the corners and points. Then tear the tissue paper away. When the work is finished, remove the tacking (basting) stitches.

*Method 4*–A really spontaneous method of transferring, well suited to appliqué, consists of cutting out (or tearing) the shapes from paper; they can be moved about upon the background until a satisfactory result is obtained, then they are pinned in place. Next, tack (baste) around the edges, again making back-stitches at corners and points. Be sure to mark the direction of the grain of the background fabric upon the paper, before removing. Later, these paper shapes will be used as the templates from which the material will be cut for the applied pieces (see chapter 5).

*Method 5*–For speed and simplicity, dressmakers' carbon paper

Fig 22 *Flowers* by Peter Brown, first-year textile student. Pink materials applied to a yellow ground, with hand and machine stitching

can be placed face down upon the background material; the tracing, or even the design itself, is put over this, and outlined with a very sharp point. (There is no reason why just key points should not be marked.) The same process can be used for the shapes which are to be applied. One disadvantage is that the lines and marks are permanent, and this limits subsequent development. Another disadvantage is that pressure upon the carbon produces marking; this is a risk when used by children.

*Method 6* – For transparent materials, outline the design in black ink; put it under the fabric, which should be held out taut, either with pins, or by framing up and supporting with books underneath. Then draw in the outline on the fabric, using a hard pencil with a very sharp point. Alternatively, mark just the key points.

When practicable, and you have the confidence to do so, there are tremendous advantages in eliminating the process of transferring, and cutting out the actual shapes directly in fabric and arranging them upon the ground material.

Inevitably an immovable line may come between inspired creative development and technical realization. This risk has to be weighed against an accurate translation of a prepared design when deciding upon the most suitable method of transferring: remember that it is simply a guide, and not an end in itself.

# 5 Creating in appliqué

## Methods and types

There are several quite distinct techniques or ways of approaching appliqué, and each gives or adds certain characteristics to the finished appearance of the work. It is up to you to decide which method will best express what you are striving to say through your design. The ability to foresee which technique to employ becomes easier with experience. It is my intention here to set out clearly, stage by stage, the actual technical processes, in such a way that even a beginner can follow the instructions. They may prove useful, but may be disregarded if they are felt to be restricting.

The influence of fashion stresses different approaches from time to time, and emphasis changes; in consequence certain aspects are ignored and others taken up and enormously explored and extended; this is happening to appliqué now. These imaginative and interesting variants will be developed under separate headings.

Once again, it must be made very clear that with the confidence born of experience you will come to use your own judgement in adapting the appliqué methods to suit your own needs and to express your own ideas.

## Simple beginnings – the direct spontaneous method

For those without previous experience or whose interest tends towards creating in colour and texture rather than actual stitchery, and also for children, this is the most straightforward way to make a start, and the most enjoyable.

1 You will either have the idea for what you want to do fairly clearly in your mind, or the scraps of material will suggest the design (see chapter 1).

2 Choose your background fabric: it should be firm, not loosely woven, and neither too thick nor too thin. When the appliqué is to be small, avoid a 'knobbly' surface. A strongly printed or woven pattern makes development difficult as it is too strident as a background; but though a large pattern is unsuitable, a small all-over patterning can be delightful.

Amongst the recommended fabrics are linens, Viyella, felt, fine suiting, fine dress-weight tweeds, flannel, gingham, denim, also many dress and lightweight furnishing (upholstery) fabrics. Then there are all the materials woven from man-made fibres: these mixtures are admirable.

It might be found helpful at this stage to refer to the selection of colour discussed in chapter 1.

Fig 23  Pieces of patterned fabric, suggesting the design
Fig 24  Cut out the pieces freely

3   Cut the background piece at least $1\frac{1}{2}$ ins larger than the finished size. It is advisable to plan for the selvedge grain of the material to run down the length of the work. The weft will then run across.

Exceptions are justified when some characteristic of the weave or patterning will add to the interest, in spite of the fact that there are technical advantages in keeping the selvedge running down. For example, little narrow stripes would probably look much better across the background, rather than downwards.

4   The choice of subject may come to you by looking through your pieces; a scrap of gold and red may make you think of a crown, another the mantle for a king; and so you build it up (fig. 23). Or you may have a preconceived idea of what you want to do. Whichever it is, select your pieces, relating the colours to the background.

There is real fun in finding just the right piece. For example, a tiny diaper-patterned printed cotton may be perfect for the roof of a decorative house or lodge; all sorts of lime and blueish-green triangles superimposed one on top of another to suggest trees might lead to an interesting mystical forest (fig. 24). Or a little patterned piece cries out to be used as the dome of some fantastic building. In your excitement, remember to avoid fabrics which will fray too much. Press the pieces with an iron on the wrong side.

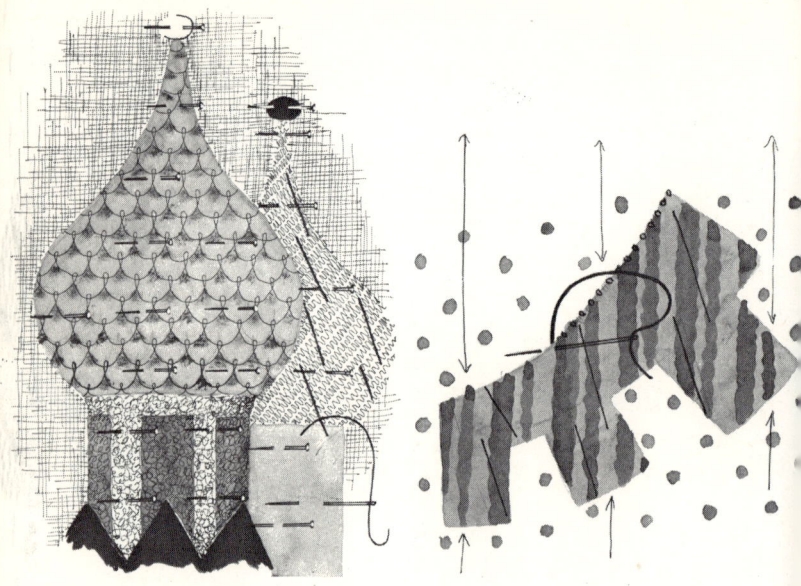

Fig 25   Starting with the pieces furthest back, pin, then tack (baste) into position

Fig 26   Take small straight stitches down into the edge of the freely cut shape

5   Cut out your shapes free-hand. Try to see that the grain of the material runs straight downwards through the shapes, but do not let this preoccupy your mind so that the freedom and spirit is lost. (This is not the method to employ if you want a carefully finished result.) It is important to capture your idea and to get it cut out.

6   Taking first the shapes which go at the back of your design or picture, pin them on to the background, keeping all the pins pointing horizontally, as this helps to keep the work flat (fig. 25). If the fabric is bulky, cut it away where it is underneath another piece.

7   It is better to tack (baste) downwards as shown in the diagram, rather than around the shapes, as this tends to cause them to rise up in the middle.

8   Using matching threads, take small, straight stitches, bringing your needle up through the background and down into the piece being applied. Sew all round the shapes (fig. 26).

This direct spontaneous approach best preserves the inspiration and most quickly converts it into terms of fabric. The lack of durability can be compensated for by superimposing decorative hand or machine embroidery (see chapters 6 and 8).

Fig 27  *Three Kings* by Frances Parker (a detail of which is shown in colour on the cover). Inspired by a printed fabric which suggested the heads; old samples and odds and ends of patterned cottons, exports to Africa and Jamaica, also metal fabric, gold kid, rug wool (yarn), etc.

Fig 28 *Purple sun 2* by Jan Beaney. Applied fabrics, wool (yarn) and cotton threads, couching, raised chain band, needle weaving, knots and straight stitches

To cut out shapes spontaneously comes naturally to children; just as they choose colours and create compositions unselfconciously, so they can and do make really lovely unsophisticated pictures and decorations in this simple method of appliqué, which appeals even to very young children. Their enjoyment is increased if they use adhesive (which will be invisible when dry), and as skill develops more stitchery will both replace the adhesive and add to the effect. (For examples of children's work see figs 29 and 51.)

**Cut paper shapes – another creative approach to appliqué**

Cut or torn paper shapes have an affinity with cut fabric and embroidery which a line drawing or design in some other medium

Fig 29  Part of a group project worked by pupils of Haggerston School, London E.2, and intended for a local day nursery

may lack. Many are the embroiderers whose courage deserts them when they attempt to design on paper, and the result is timid and too small in scale; yet with scissors and coloured paper they will cut interesting shapes which can subsequently be manipulated upon the background until a satisfactory composition emerges. These cut paper forms are then replaced by fabrics chosen for their colour, tone and texture.

1   Select the background fabric for the appliqué, pin (tack) it out, (or up) so that it is taut. If it is going to be framed up, follow directions on pages 23-6, either for the fabric or the backing. Have the frame slightly slack.

2   Collect together papers of different tones and textures. Decide upon the subject matter of the design; the idea may come in several ways, from vegetation, wood graining, pebbles, buildings,

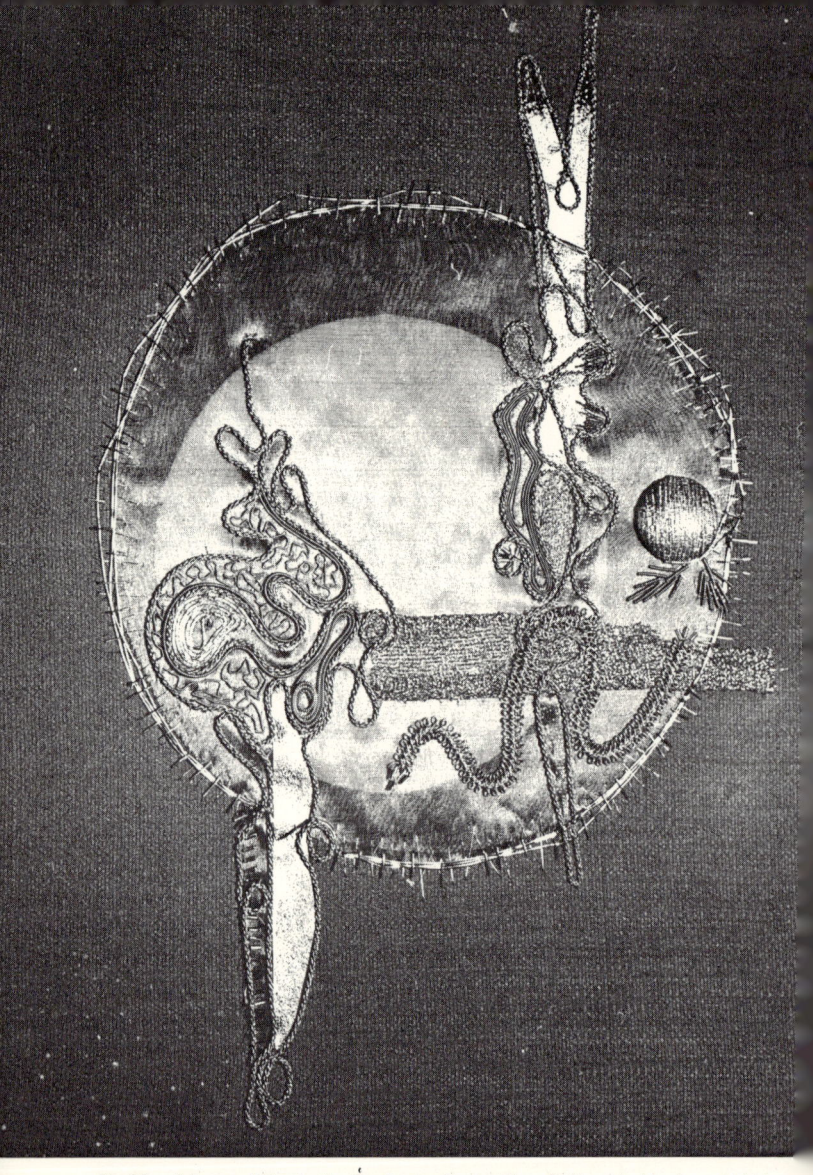

Fig 30 *Adam and Eve in the Garden* by Bucky King. Dull golds, blacks, gold kid, metal threads, wire mesh, etc., applied to dark, black-gold ground fabric

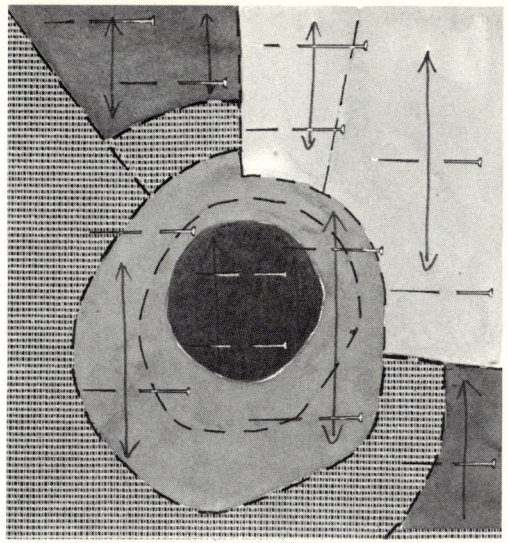

Fig 31 Cutting out the shapes spontaneously and arranging them on the background

animals, vases, etc. It can be built up from abstract or geometric shapes or evolve from bits and pieces of fabric or the paper you have collected. Cut out or tear interesting and varied shapes from the different papers, making sure that they are large enough in scale for the size of the background area.

3   Arrange these shapes upon the background, moving them around until you attain the balance and rhythm which you aim to achieve, then pin them in place.

4   On the background, tack (baste) around each shape. To prevent puckering should be your constant aim, so mark in the direction of the grain of the background upon each paper piece. Also mark in the outline of the overlapping shapes (fig. 31).

5   Choose just the right scraps of fabric for each shape, watching the tone values, colour and texture, and 'using', in the decorative sense, the characteristics of printed or woven patterns (to get the most interesting effect it may be necessary to use these 'off' grain). Transparent nets and gauzes give unexpected results when they overlap.

6   Remove each paper template and put it upon the chosen piece of fabric, making sure that the lines indicating the grain (drawn on the paper pieces) correspond with the grain of the scrap of fabric, where applicable. Tack (baste) around the outline (fig. 32).

7   To prevent fraying, where necessary, iron on Vilene to the back of the pieces of fabric (fig. 33).

8   Cut out, either exactly on the line or leaving a turning for blind appliqué (refer to treatment of edges, pages 42, 45 and 55).

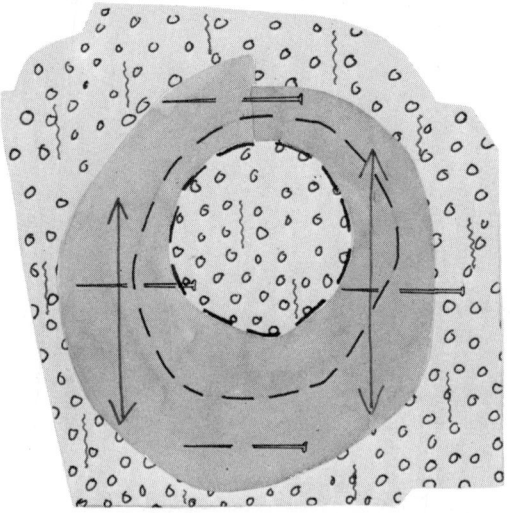

Fig 32 Remove each paper template and pin it on the selected piece of fabric, matching up the grain

Fig 33 Vilene (Pellon) or Stayflex cut to the finished shape and ironed on to the back of the piece of fabric, will make it easier to bend over the lay after snipping; then tack and press before pinning to the background. Alternatively, the Vilene (Pellon) can cover the turnings as well, to prevent fraying

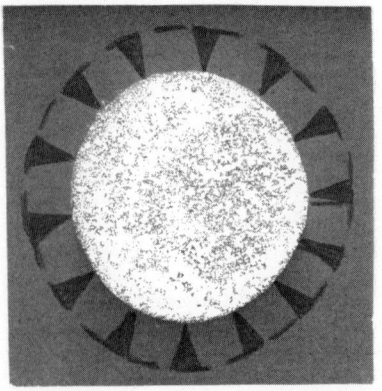

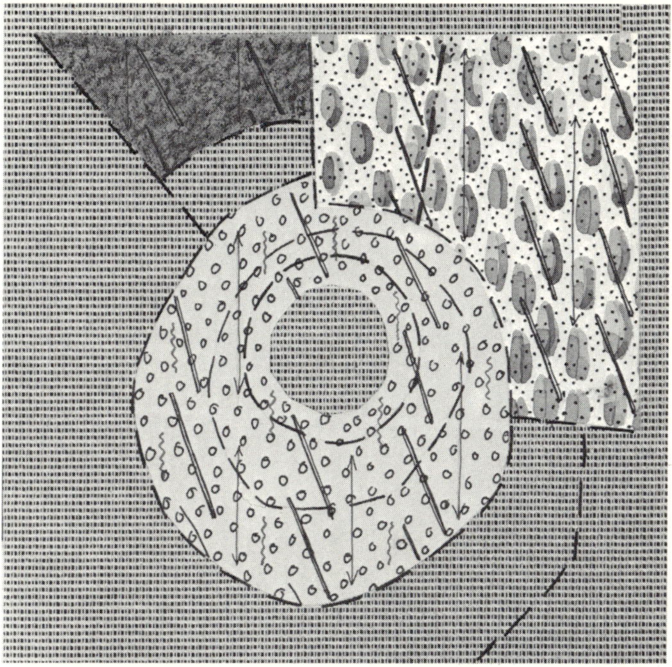

Fig 34   Pin, then tack (baste) to the background the fabric pieces to be applied, starting with the ones underneath. Here the edges are cut to the outline except where they will lie underneath another piece

Fig 35   Dealing with turnings on curves: snip, bend over and tack (baste), before applying to the background

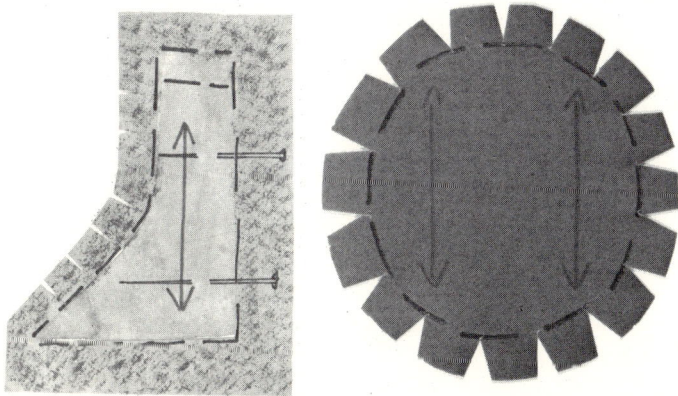

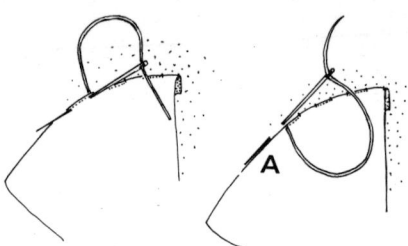

Fig 36  Slip-stitching. Slip the needle through the edge of the fold, bring it out, then take it through the background fabric, as at A. Repeat

Unless the materials are very thin or are transparent, cut away the surplus (leaving about $\frac{1}{2}$ in.) on the parts which will lie underneath other pieces (fig. 34). (But if you feel that you may want to make alterations, then do not cut away.)
9  Where there is to be a turned-in edge, snip the turning on the concave curves and at corners, and nick out little pieces at intervals on convex curves (fig. 35).
10  Starting with the shapes which are to go underneath, put each in place and zig-zag tack (baste) vertically, ending with those on top (fig. 34).
11  Bringing the needle up through the background and taking it down through the applied piece, make tiny straight stitches into the edge, or hem it. For blind appliqué, slip-stitching can be used (fig. 36). If a frame has been used it can be tightened up either before or after this stage.
12  The design can now be developed further with surface stitchery, etc. (see chapters 6 and 8).

There are several advantages to this appliqué method, the main one being that the creating is done directly in paper or fabric, and, as it can be changed as the work proceeds, the liveliness is preserved. And it is specially well suited for very large projects such as hangings, stage curtains, dossals, room-dividers, window curtains, panels, etc.

### Appliqué – the basic method

When accuracy and a good professional finish are necessary, or repetition is required, this conventional formula is the most reliable, and the result makes it well worth following. But this tells you *how* to do it, not *what* to do.

The formal technical processes are often doubted nowadays, and it is sometimes thought that to recommend care in preparation will result in dullness and lack of vitality, and that the dynamic approach will be lost. But this is a personal matter; some instinctive designers are put off by formality, they are the individualists

Fig 37 *Civic dignity* worked by Letitia Lambert. Thai silk, tones of red on brilliant blue and purple. Gold embroidered decoration inspired by units cut from paper doileys glued on the original design

who create directly in fabric, and have to work spontaneously. For them, this method would be too tiresome. So, in this instance, if technical perfection is sacrificed, something far more important may be gained.

You should never allow technique to become an end in itself, or place too much reliance upon following a formula instead of letting the imagination work and using common sense; but the following instructions are set out clearly in the hope that by working to a planned order, some really good idea may lose nothing during the process of its realization and that puckering may be

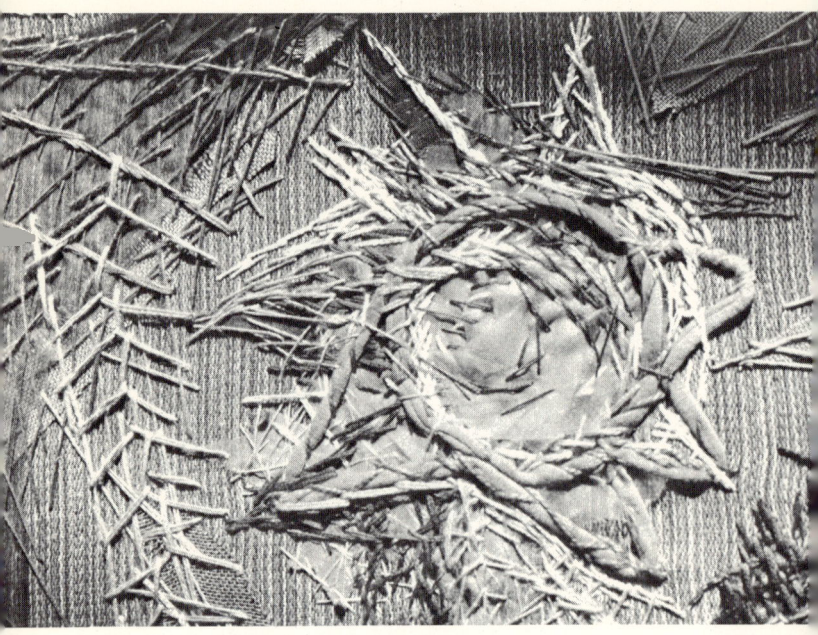

Fig 38  Detail of stitchery *Galaxy* by Nik Krevitsky. Appliqués of linen, transparent silk and cotton, jersey fabrics, stitched to cotton ground

prevented, instead of trusting to the final stretching as a cure for all discrepancies.

1   Draw out the design to full size, or have the sketch photographically blown up.
2   Select and frame up the background fabric (see page 23).
3   Tighten up the frame, and support the fabric by putting books or something flat underneath, to give a firm surface for painting.
4   Mark the selvedge grain of the fabric on the perforated tracing (fig. 40). Put the perforated tracing in place on the fabric, using weights to keep it from moving. Pounce, and paint on the design, as described on pages 28-9
5   With the whole design area exposed and the frame slightly slack (longer side slats may be necessary), choose the pieces of material to be applied, pin them in place temporarily, then prop the frame up and look at it critically from a distance.

Judge whether you have distributed the tones to produce the effect at which you are aiming: is there a centre of interest?. (It should avoid the actual centre.) Have you an interesting balance?

Fig 39 Plan the colours and tones

Has the best possible use been made of texture and transparency? Have the colours been arranged so that they bring out all that is best in the design? By altering the grouping, quite different results can be obtained; and by adjustment a design can be made 'readable'; or, if it is abstract, a change of emphasis by shifting the colours around can alter the pattern. For example, with the arrangement of tone shown in fig. 39, a vignette is formed which concentrates the interest. The opposite is the outcome when tones and colours are too diverse and spotted all over the area.

6 When a satisfactory arrangement of the pieces of fabric has been planned, decide the order in which each piece should be applied to the background and mark this on the tracing (fig. 40), starting with the one at the back, or underneath.

7 According to the design, the materials, and the scale of the whole thing (and sometimes the purpose), you will know whether you want to leave cut edges, or turned-in edges (blind appliqué) which gives a harder, definite edge, and is more durable. There is no reason why both should not be combined on the same piece

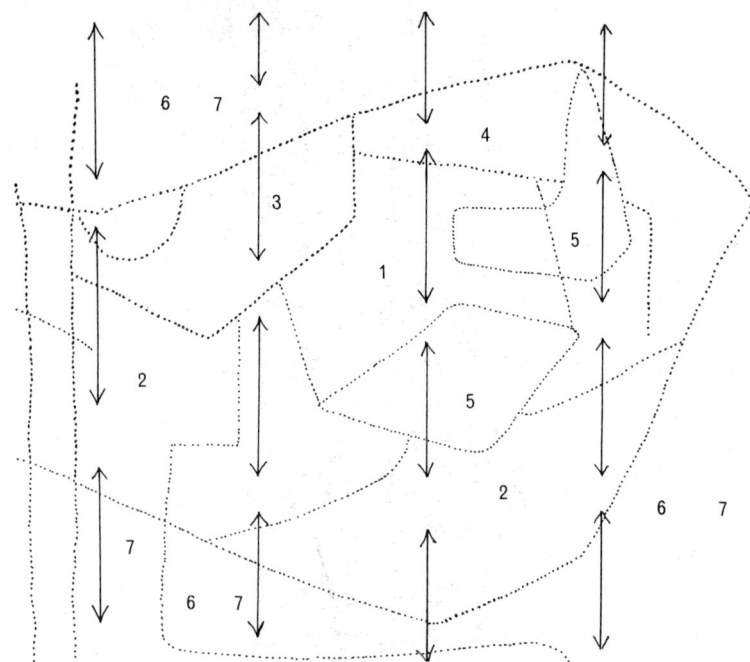

Fig 40  Mark the selvedge grain of the fabric on the perforated tracing, and mark the order in which each piece should be applied to the background material

of work, and as you gain experience you will be able to decide about this as the work progresses.

8  One by one, pin out each piece of fabric on a board with drawing pins (thumbtacks), making sure that the selvedge grain runs downwards so that it will correspond with the background (fig. 41). This is important because the tension is then the same, and the fabric is much less likely to pucker. (But, as has been said before, this can be disregarded when there is some good reason for doing so: for example, a scrap of striped material may look right when placed diagonally, or a ribbed silk be more effective used vertically instead of horizontally.)

Then put the appropriate area of the tracing over the piece of material, pounce and paint or spray, flick away the surplus pounce, and remove the drawing pins (thumbtacks). Repeat this for each piece.

9  Cut out each piece, leaving about $\frac{1}{2}$ in. where another shape will overlap, and cut close to the outside edge, or leave a narrow turning as required (fig. 42).

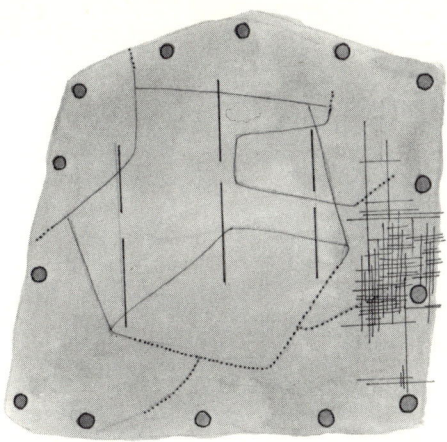

Fig 41  One by one, pin out each piece, with the selvedge grain running downwards. Trace and paint on the lines

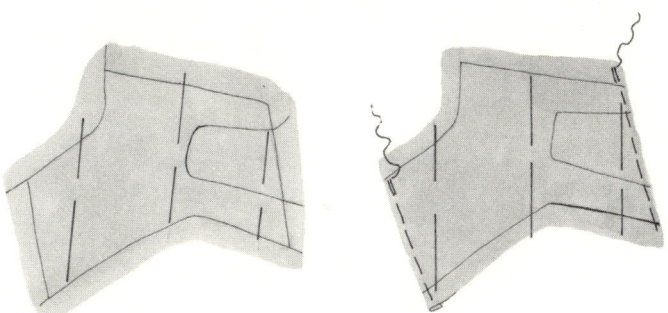

Fig 42  Cut each piece to the desired shape, leaving about ½ in. where another shape will overlap. Leave a turning or cut to the edge where necessary

Fig 43  Turn under the edges, where necessary, and tack (baste)

For intricate shapes the thinnest Vilene (Pellon) or Stayflex can be ironed over the back of the whole piece (if the material is not too thin) to prevent fraying; or just the shape, excluding turnings, can be reinforced: to do this, reverse the tracing and transfer it to the Vilene; cut on this line and iron on, then cut the fabric of the piece to be applied, leaving turnings (fig. 33). Snip and turn down the lay on the edges (figs 35 and 43).

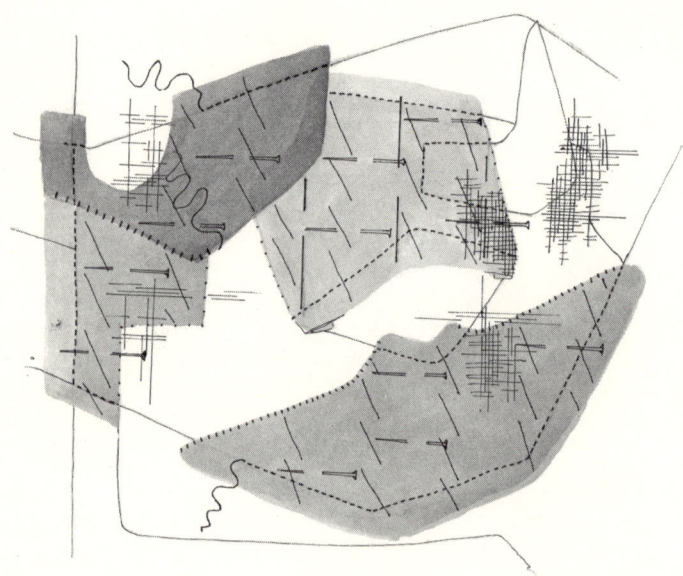

Fig 44 Starting with piece No. 1 (see fig. 40), pin, tack (baste) and run-stitch along the traced lines where they will be covered by subsequent pieces. Slip stitch or hem the outside edges

10 Starting with the underneath fabric, pin, tack (baste) and stitch to the background one by one (fig. 44), until the final fabric shape or shapes on top have been sewn on. In fig. 39, note how a piece of opaque fabric (No. 6 in fig. 40) has been lightly stitched in place before being covered by the transparent material.

Usually, but not necessarily, this sewing-down is done with the frame very slightly slack. Now tighten up the frame, if it is of a size which can be reached for further sewing. Otherwise, roll in (i.e. roll the material round the top, bottom or both rollers; this can be released as the work is completed) to a convenient size before tightening up.

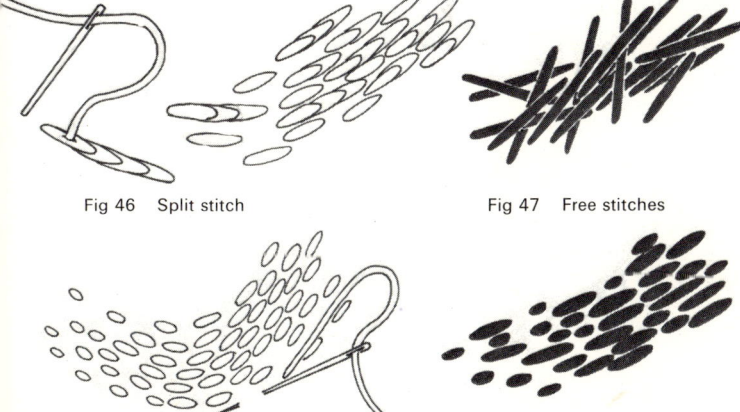

Fig 45  Stitched textures

Fig 46  Split stitch

Fig 47  Free stitches

Fig 48  Running stitches, and running stitches of unequal lengths

Fig 49 *Red rising* by Joy Clucas. Applied fabric and machine stitching in tones of red. This is an example of soft broken edges (see also fig. 54)

This completes the preparation, and the appliqué is now ready to be developed with surface stitchery.

Fig. 45 shows some ways of producing broken edges and surface textures; for example, split-stitch (fig. 46). Here the needle is shown having been brought up through the previous stitch and being taken down into the fabric ahead: it is better to use a frame. Other possibilities include long straight stitches at random (fig. 47) and running and irregular running stitches (fig. 48).

The precision and reliability of this method of appliqué makes it specially suitable for banners, alter-frontals, pairs of curtains, etc., and also for work which has to be repeated many times, as for much professional and commercial work. The disadvantages are

Fig 50 Detail of round stitchery *Cavern* by Nik Krevitsky. Appliqués of silk-screen printed fabrics and silk on ground of fabric of mixed fibres

that there is the painted line, and there is little chance of changing anything.

With experience it will be found that this process can be varied without serious consequences. For example, if you prefer not to use a frame, it is possible to keep the work flat by having the background pinned out or kept taut with weights.

For very large pieces of work (unless a huge frame is used or the method illustrated in fig. 14 is adopted), a certain amount of manipulation has to take place. For example, the background material can be tacked to laths, top and bottom: the top can be suspended from the ceiling, and then raised and lowered as required by means of ropes and pulleys.

Fig 51 Three examples by pupils from Haggerston School, London E.2. Top left, in blues and greens. Top right, browns and yellow on light blue. Bottom, dark green and blue with bright pink

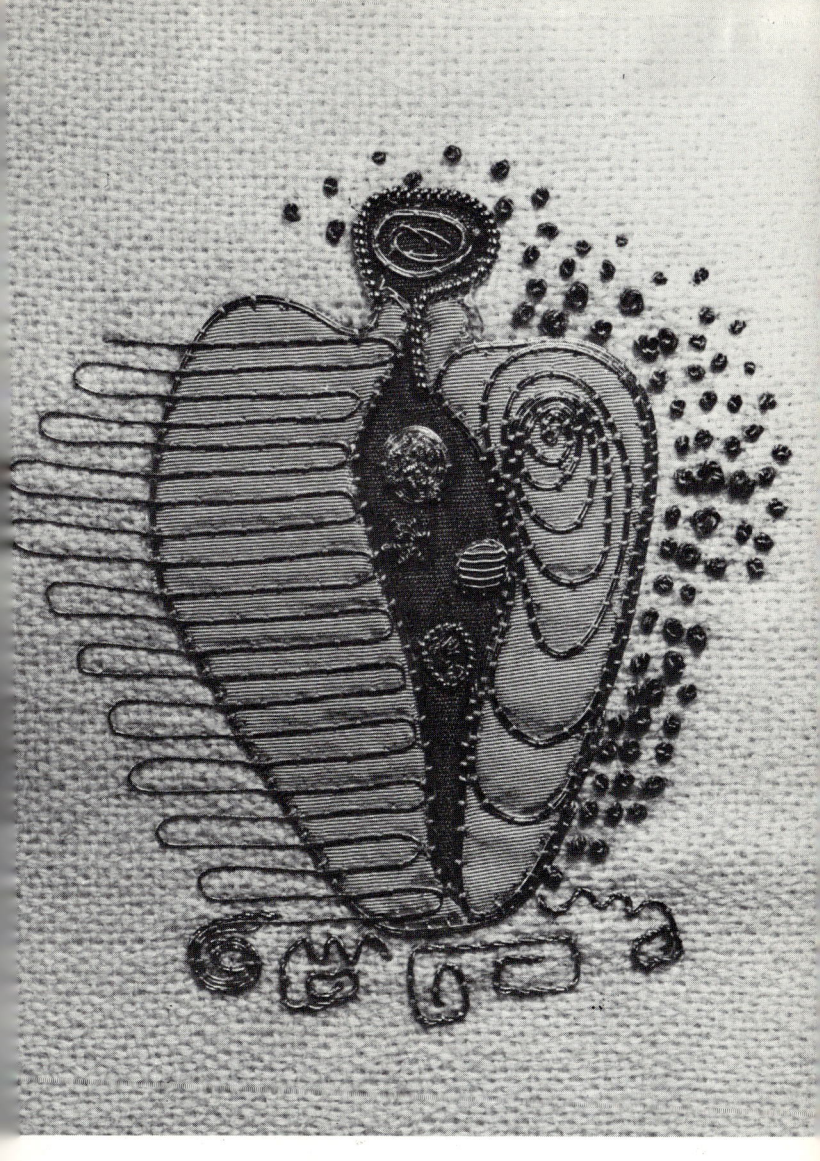

Fig 52 Detail, showing appliqué enriched with French knots and couched metal threads

# 6 Further techniques

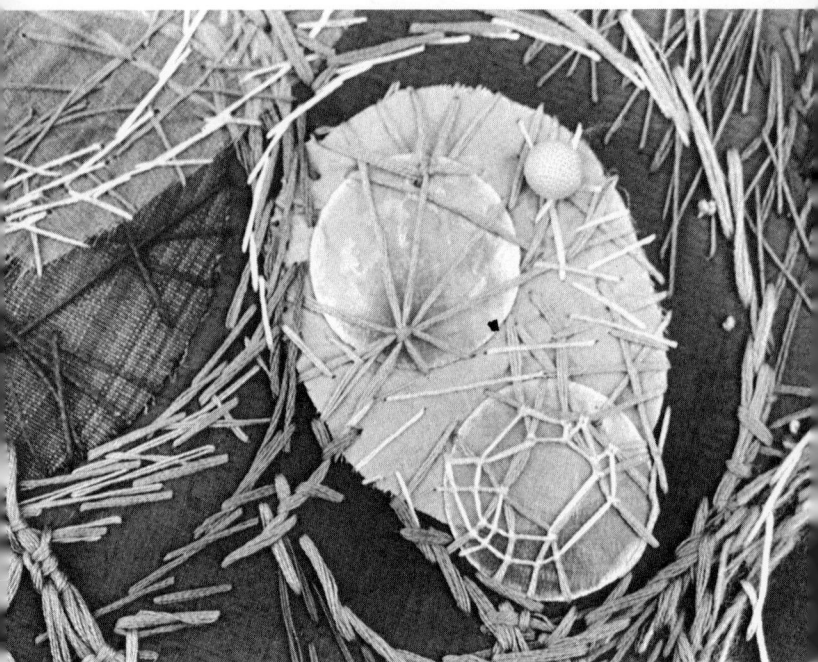

Fig 53  *Moonscape* (detail) by Nik Krevitsky. Appliqués in wool, linen, silk with translucent capiz shells and cloth-covered buttons

## Surface stitchery in relation to appliqué

Where the applied shapes are intrinsically good, appliqué and blind appliqué can be satisfying without the addition of stitchery; but over the years the changes of balance have come and gone according to the current mood of expression. Satin applied to velvet interpreted the counterchange patterns which only required a cording around the edges. Then towards the end of the nineteenth century and onwards the style characteristic of the Glasgow school had a tremendous influence; it was usual to find linen or crêpe-de-chine applied to linen, a slanting satin stitch covered all outlines, other lines were worked in stem stitch.

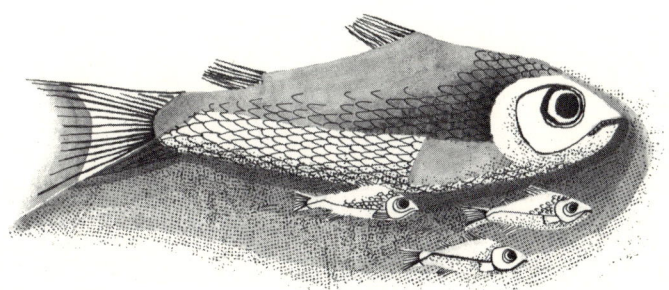

Fig 54  The soft, broken edge

Later, as a reaction to this, a degree of freedom hitherto unknown was introduced. A wider variety of fabrics were cut out and used spontaneously; edges were simply hemmed down and the line was emphasized where necessary with, for example, herringbone stitch, interlaced herringbone, etc. Surface filling stitches, buttons, sequins, ribbons and veiling were incorporated into the design; the impact made by these innovations is still being felt, especially, perhaps, in the use of transparent materials.

The vogue for the 'slipped' outline has been interpreted in embroidery by superimposing linear stitchery upon areas of flat, opaque or transparent colour. Contrasted with this is the softness of the edge which is lost and obliterated by layers of net or merged into the background by applying other translucent materials, using invisible thread and tiny stitches (fig. 54). Areas of texture are produced by working French knots, detached chain stitches, etc., and by using 'knobbly' fabrics. Line stitches which can be varied in width are important, such as Cretan, Pekinese, etc. These and many other adaptable stitches (figs 55–57) are invaluable, and have become an integral characteristic of mid-twentieth-century appliqué, and the photographs of work reproduced in this book should be studied with a view to seeing how and why these methods have been introduced.

With the flowing rhythmic movement and the ornamental play of line inherent in the current Art Nouveau revival, it seems inevitable that the emphasis may again be upon the significance and decorative value of line independent of the content. In consequence, non-fraying, smooth fabric such as felt, PVC, and thin leathers will be used in conjunction with couching various cords and braids which have to be sewn over, into or through (fig. 57).

Fig 55  Stitches to produce a broken surface
**A**  French knots (keep the thumb over the twist as the thread is pulled through)
**B**  detached chain stitches
**C**  seeding (a small back stitch covered with another)

Fig 56  Stitches to produce variation and irregularities of width
**A**  backstitch, worked from right to left
**B**  Pekinese
**C**  Open chain
**D**  Cretan

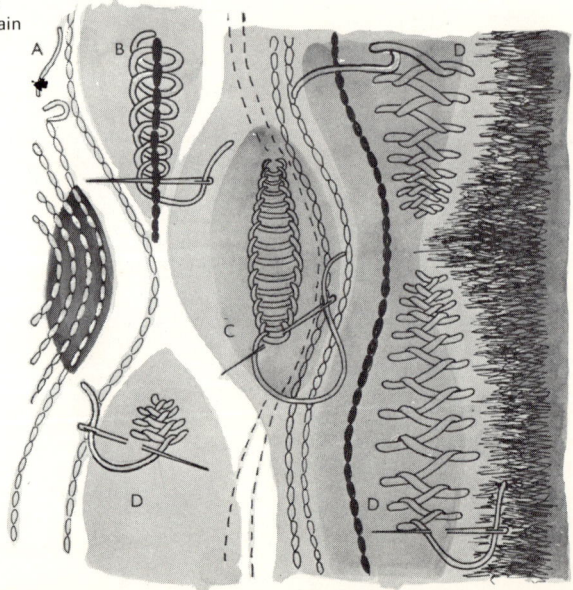

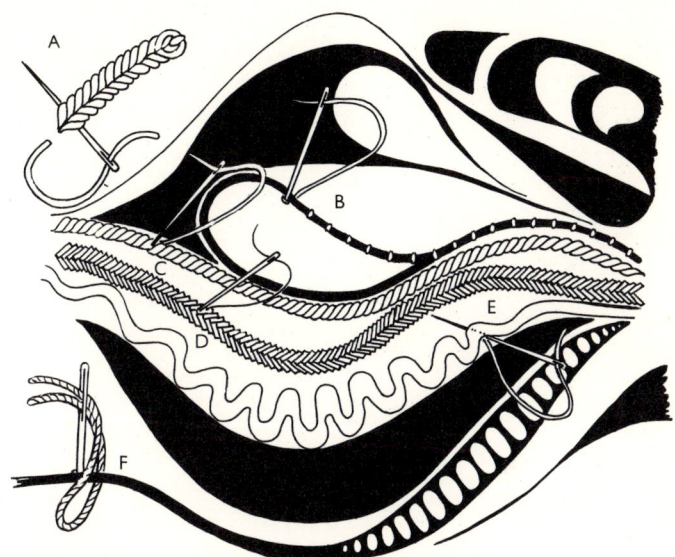

Fig 57 Lines
A heavy chain stitch (start with one small back stitch)
B couching – one thick thread, or several finer threads, sewn over with a small stitch
C sewing down a cord, with a slanting stitch taken into the twist
D sewing down a plait
E for a tubular braid, sew through from side to side
F taking the cords etc. through to the back with a chenille needle and sling

A fine needle and invisible thread or waxed silk can be used. At the beginning and end, cut the braid or cord, leaving at least $\frac{1}{2}$ in., and take it through to the back. Make a hole with a stiletto, and use a large chenille needle threaded with a thick thread doubled to form a loop, to help to pull the ends of cord through (fig. 57); they can then be flattened and pasted back. To keep a good line the use of an embroidery frame is recommended; even a tambour (drum) frame (fig. 59) may be sufficient, particularly when executing the surface stitchery if the appliqué has been done in the hand.

## Appliqué in limited colour – practical uses

Exploring the possibilities of appliqué carried out in white only, or in monotone, is most interesting, and need not imply a lack of variety. It depends mainly upon the arrangement of texture and degree of contrast between transparency and opaqueness.

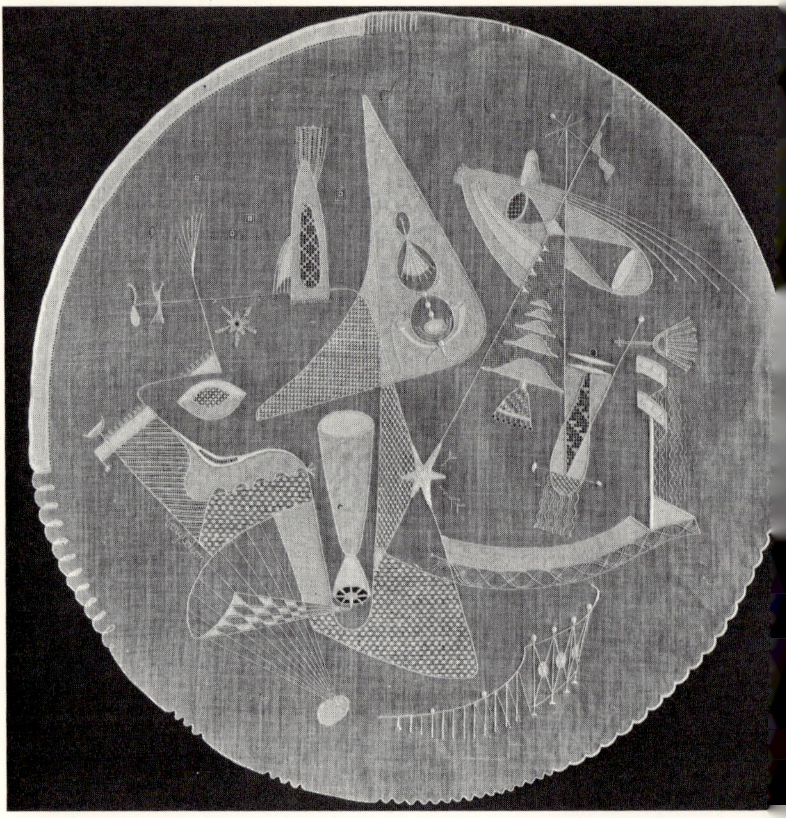

Fig 58 *Festival* (1957) by Beryl Dean. Very fine hand white-work intended to be mounted between two thicknesses of Perspex (Plexiglas) as a coffee table top

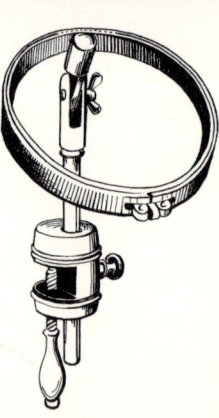

Fig 59  A clamp-on tambour (drum) frame

Try accepting this limitation and work out a series of experiments; you will become fascinated.

Remembering that what is said about white work applies equally to neutral tones and to colour, let us next consider the practical purposes for which this kind of appliqué can be used:

For the house, on tablecloths, place mats, tray and trolley cloths, guest towels, curtains, household linen, etc., and special pieces intended for mounting between two layers of glass or perspex (Plexiglas) (fig. 58).

For children's and baby clothes, dresses, blouses and aprons for all ages, accessories, lingerie, etc.

For church altar linen, fair linen and credence cloths, palls, corporals, lavabo towels and purificators (fig. 60).

This form of appliqué must be strong enough to withstand laundering. The method is often considered entirely unsuitable, but it need not be eliminated if certain points are observed:

1 All the textiles (and threads) used must be washable and unlikely to fray. Fig. 60 shows a very fine opaque linen applied to a slightly open hand-woven linen.

2 Keep to fairly small areas of appliqué and try to design so that the surface stitchery holds the two together.

3 Take special care that the pieces to be applied correspond in tension and grain with the background. The preparation already described for conventional and blind appliqué should be carried out.

4 The treatment of the edges must be strong. Pin-stitching is very satisfactory; fig. 61 shows how it is done: use a fine thread and a needle size 7 or 8, working on the right side of the article, from right to left. The finished result can be seen surrounding the outside of the smaller applied squares in fig. 60. Three-sided stitch (punch stitch) for which the edge need not be turned in, is seldom used now.

Man-made and synthetic textiles, such as nylon, can be used in addition to chiffon, organdie, and linen lawn.

There are delightful examples of semi-opaque lawn or cambric hemmed to an almost transparent muslin from India; and the same blind appliqué is a tradition in Hungary where the ground is usually a fine cotton net (fig. 62).

*Over page*
Fig 60  One end (36 ins deep), of a fair linen cloth embroidered on hand woven linen. Beryl Dean

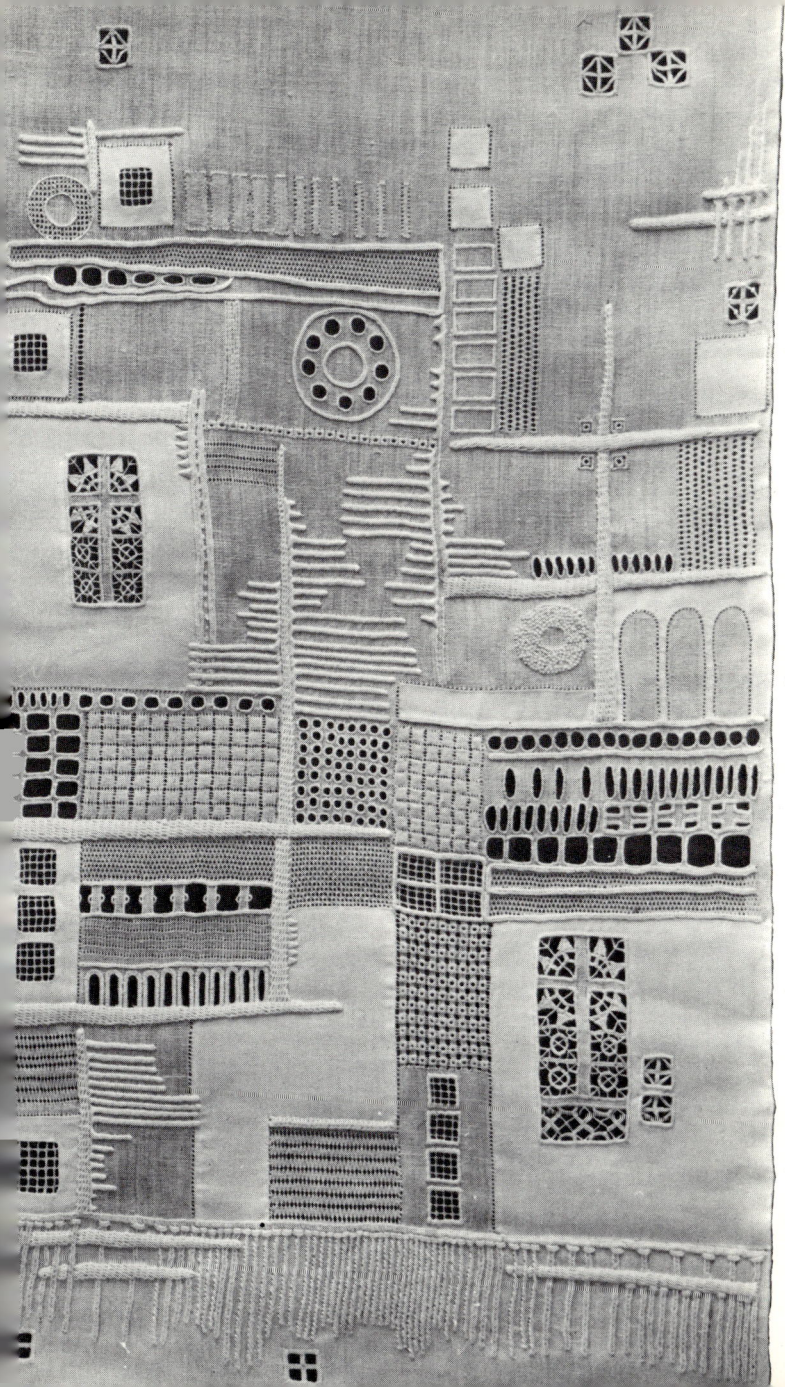

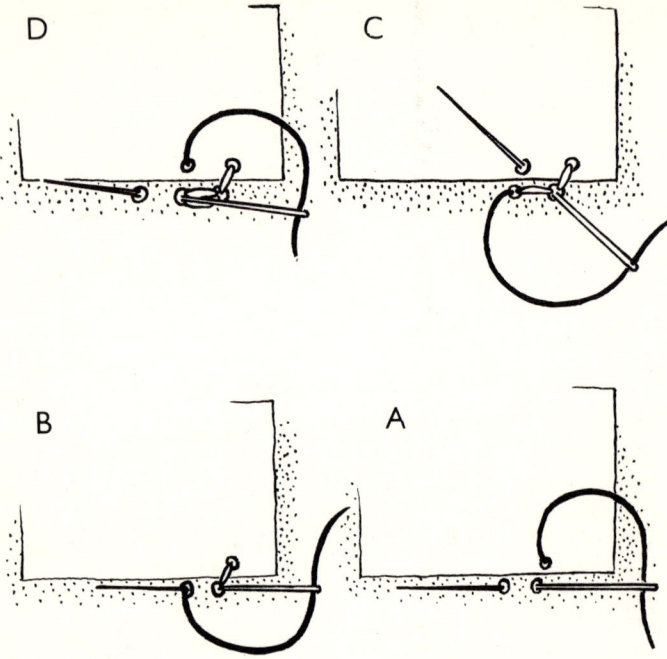

Fig 61  Pin-stitching

## Applying a semi-opaque to a transparent material

1  Draw out your design on paper, go over the outline in ink.
2  Put the cambric or linen lawn on this, and pin it out tightly. You should be able to see the line through the fabric.
3  Very lightly trace the outline of the design on to the lawn or cambric. This can be done with a sharply pointed, very hard pencil. On the diagram (fig. 63) this line is shown in larger spaced dots.
4  Then take the lawn and put it over the piece of net. Pin the two together, keeping the pins horizontal.
5  Tack (baste) all round the design, keeping about ¼ in. inside the outline. This, too, is shown on the diagram.
6  Next, insert the scissors about ⅛ in. outside the outline, being careful not to cut through to the net. Two pins, crossed, put between the two layers of fabric (A) will keep them separated whilst making the incision. Then cut along for a few inches, keeping about ⅛ in. outside the outline. At the concave curves make little snips (B) and at the convex curves cut out small nicks (C). Cut diagonally into corners.

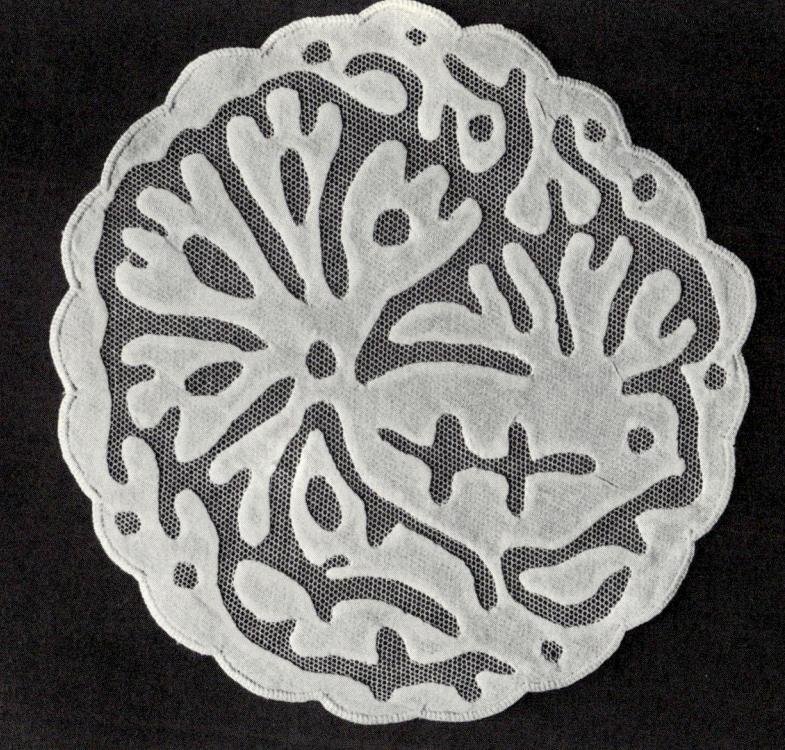

Fig 62  Blind appliqué from Hungary

7   Cut only a few inches at a time, to prevent fraying and then, with a very fine sewing thread and fine needle, turn under the $\frac{1}{8}$ in. lay with the point of the needle. This turned-in edge is shown in the diagram with a line of tiny dots close together.

8   With very small stitches, as close to the fold as possible, hem (D) until a few more inches need to be cut away. (Slip stitching could be used.)

9   In the example in fig. 62 a buttonhole stitch has been worked around the edge of the design, through the lawn and net, before cutting away the surplus.

You will see that for some of the semi-transparent shapes in fig. 58, fine cambric and linen lawns have been applied to the underside of the organdie background. To do this, an embroidery frame is recommended, especially when trailing (three or more threads sewn over with small satin stitches) is used as an outline on the surface. Upon completion, the surplus turnings are cut away on the reverse side. Very exciting variants can be produced when machine stitching is used on top (and also when contrasting colours are introduced).

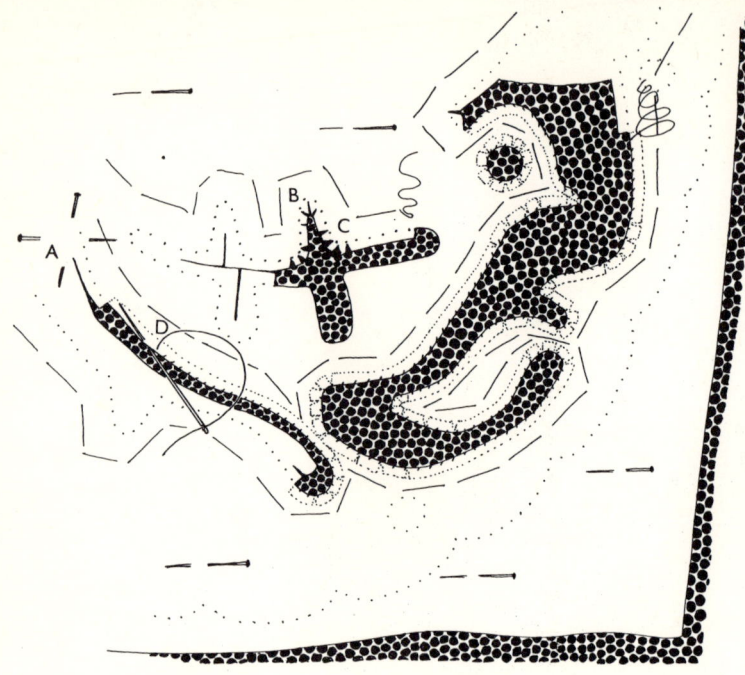

Fig 63  Blind appliqué

The foregoing surfeit of well-intentioned technical directions must not be allowed to obscure the liveliness of the medium, or the wide range of ideas which can be expressed when restricting the use of colour. The attention given to the preparation should never restrain the freedom of line.

## Lettering in appliqué

From the huge banner composed of words formed with letters quickly cut out and machine stitched upon a contrasting background, to the infinitely delicate wording worked upon a presentation prayer book cover, appliqué is an ideal medium to use because it is capable of great precision. For lettering on church banners, standards, regimental colours, official table covers and hangings, heraldry, nursery panels, rag books, initials and monograms, etc., appliqué is the most direct, accurate and (if speed is important) the quickest method to use.

Follow the technical instructions already given for the preparation. Invariably it is an advantage to back the fabric with some suitable medium such as Vilene (Pellon) (figs 33 and 35); certainly, if the edges are to be cut rather than turned in, the whole should be backed before cutting out the letters. Turned-in edges are more durable, but if the letters are small it would tend to make them clumsy and illegible. An outline of one or more cords can be used, perhaps stressing one side of the letters. For this, sew into the twist of the cord (fig. 57) and see that corners and points are kept sharp by taking a little stitch into both sides of the cord. For most styles of lettering precision should be the aim.

The importance of using really good, well spaced and proportioned alphabets cannot be over-stressed, as lettering is useless unless readable from a distance. Even when the purpose is purely decorative, choose letters suitable for appliqué. Do refer to books which deal specifically with the subject; some are listed in the bibliography at the back of this book. Realize that characters designed to be written with a quill will not lend themselves to adaptation in terms of cut fabric, nor will subtle serifs withstand the likelihood of fraying.

Fig 64 An alphabet book by Pat and Pru Russell. A variety of fabrics, appliquéd on felt; letters edged with chenille and worked out in machine embroidery

Fig 65 The words 'towards men', part of an orphrey by Pat Russell, a calligrapher, who has designed the letters to be carried out in appliqué combined with machine embroidery

Fig 66 Ancient Arabic characters from Egypt. Cotton applied to cotton in blind appliqué. The grain of the cotton material is all cut on the cross

## Padding

For padded appliqué (see fig. 67) one or more layers of felt are generally used. Transfer the tracing of the shape to be padded onto the felt so that it can be cut out accurately. Where several layers are used for a three-dimensional effect, this will be the top one, and each layer underneath should be cut slightly smaller than the one above it. They are then tacked (basted) together in position and the final layer is stitched down with closely spaced stitches before covering with fabric.

## Expressing yourself

The particular joy about appliqué is that anyone can do it; you don't need to have had previous experience or 'know how'. If you get a good idea, and you are longing to express it, go ahead, cut it out in paper or fabric, arrange it to your satisfaction upon the chosen background; add whatever you need to complete the composition, making use of those stitches which you know, and you will find you have created something which bears the imprint of your own personality. Next time you might be more ambitious. Read about the methods of work, think about them, but do not let the acquisition of technique come between you and your idea. Get it down and enjoy doing it, and you will have discovered a pleasure which is there to enrich life through your own imagina-

Fig 67  *Fish in glass case* by Ann Jackson. White and old gold on grey-green

tion. Look at the panel 'Tommy' (fig. 70); it has this quality of sincere naivety. Again, Ann Jackson experienced a feeling of satisfaction when working out her idea (fig. 67) which was a great advance on anything she had tackled before. At first she was dubious about padding up her fish, then she saw how it added to the interest. Letitia Lambert had great fun capturing and interpreting character in terms of appliqué (fig. 37); it was a challenge, and it came off: for it she used brilliant pinks and red on a ground of rich blue and purple Thai silk, which was set off by the gold bullion work and black felt outline.

'Showboat' (fig. 68), worked in 1958, came about partly as the result of studying the ingenious use of steel spangles, net and chenille in the decoration of men's court suits of the eighteenth century, and also the introduction of padding for stump-work. This coincided with the gift of a box of odd small pieces of braid, ribbon, French tape and eyelets, etc. The little panel is slightly raised away from the background; it is in black and white on mauve reversible slipper satin.

If you have not already done so, do think of a subject which interests you or maybe a possible recipient; it might be connected with a hobby, profession, collection, your garden, car or a favourite possession. Then, having found some scraps of fabric, cut out shapes connected with your choice of subject, arrange them, and at once you are creating something which has a unique personality.

Fig 68  *Showboat*, a small panel by Beryl Dean. Many experimental fabrics and braids etc., applied on the light side of slipper satin, surrounded by the reverse side

Fig 69  Book cover by Margery Stenning, Stanhope Institute, London. Appliqué, with couched metal thread surface stitchery

Fig 70  *Tommy* by Rose Hannah Holt. Various fabrics, including velvet and veiling

If your imagination has been sparked off and you are creating your own appliqué, then the purpose of this book has been fulfilled.

# 7 Decoration as part of construction— practical uses

Fig 71 Canopy of a hackney carriage, from Bombay. Blind appliqué, with yellow, brown, red and white cotton applied to a dark blue cotton ground. Victoria and Albert Museum

Appliqué can be used in both aesthetic and practical ways; and for practical uses an effect can be obtained fairly quickly, should this be the aim.

The degree of durability will depend largely on the technique employed and the materials used. For example, cushion covers get considerable wear, and have to be cleaned frequently, as do all types of hand, shopping, work and carrying bags. Bedspreads, curtains, hangings, etc., have to withstand everyday use. For all of these blind appliqué is generally the most practical method, and the limitations imposed by designing for a purpose, or to fit the construction of an object, provide the individuality which gives added charm. Look, for instance, at the examples from India shown in figs 71 and 72.

Fig 72  Bihari hood. Blind appliqué, with white, red, and yellow cotton applied to black linen. Victoria and Albert Museum

Deliberately to design around some part of the construction will make a feature of it, as for shaped caps, accessories, decoration at necklines, hems, sleeve ends and zipper openings on dresses, the examples from India might inspire designs to be used in this way.

When machine embroidery is combined with appliqué (see page 74), again some detail of the construction of, for instance, a garment can become the centre of interest, such as pockets on aprons and clothes, especially on young children's wear (fig. 73). Another dress, from Switzerland, made from towelling (terry-cloth), had a large central pocket in a contrasting colour, with appliquéd machine-stitched flowers springing from it.

The aesthetic approach can be specially appreciated when used

Fig 73 Children's dresses. Left, yellow with applied pink towelling (terrycloth) apple as pocket. Right, dark blue with white and red towelling applied

Fig 74 *Poppies* by Kathleen Whyte. A room divider. The elusive quality is achieved by overlaying transparent fabrics of brilliant reds and pinks, with a minimum of stitchery

Fig 75 Cushion by Ann Bowles, in greens, blue, mauve etc.—appliqué combined with machine embroidery

for light transparent curtains, lampshades, and room dividers; the translucency of Kathleen Whyte's exquisite 'Poppies' is a good example (fig. 74).

In complete contrast is appliqué with thin leathers on PVC, possibly incorporating wool or felt. A rubber-based adhesive helps in the preparation. Both machine and hand stitching can be used, and there are endless experiments which can be tried out, such as cutting holes to reveal shisha glass (small pieces of glass seen in Indian embroidery). Bags of all types, shoes, slippers, stool tops, glove-boxes, pouffes, garments, cushions, etc., can all be designed with decoration which depends upon the line of the construction.

This applies also to really large hangings, curtains, cloaks, etc., which will be considered in chapter 9.

# 8 Machine embroidered and stitched appliqué

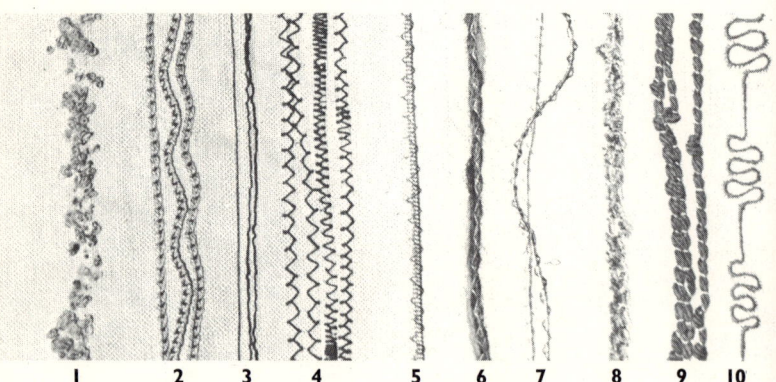

Fig 76  Machine stitching
**1** moss stitch **2** chain stitch **3** plain stitch, varying lengths **4** zig-zag, varying widths of stitch **5** zig-zag used for couching braid **6** zig-zag used for couching thick wool **7** zig-zag couching single thread **8** cable stitch, chenille **9** cable stitch, Anchor soft **10** whip stitch

There are immense creative possibilities in appliqué carried out entirely by machine stitching or combined with hand work. There are many different sewing machines available, but it is surprising how much can be done with an ordinary domestic machine. Mechanical adjustments are made according to the type of machine and the technique and stitches required, but this lies outside the scope of this book and you should refer to the reading list on page 103 for further information.

If the directly spontaneous approach appeals to you and you enjoy experimenting with the minimum of preparation, you can simply cut out fabric shapes and machine-stitch them to the background. Stronger lines and textures can then be added. A better technical finish results from following the basic method of preparation suggested for hand-worked appliqué on page 44, and the advice upon the choice of material remains the same.

Because of the nature of machine work there are certain differences, which in the main are as follows:

Usually only the main lines of the design are tacked (basted) or marked on the fabric, as it is a characteristic that as much as possible should be free-hand. Sometimes it is necessary to work on the wrong side, for example, when working cable stitch; in this case the design is traced on to the reverse of the backing or muslin.

The pieces to be applied are generally cut with turnings allowed, and these are trimmed away after stitching.

To prevent puckering the work is held in an embroidery hoop, which can be moved as required. Paper or vanishing muslin can also be used under the work to keep it flat; paper can be torn away afterwards, and vanishing muslin is removed by pressing with a hot iron.

Fig. 76 shows some of the embroidery stitches which can be worked on a sewing machine.

Where a line or an edge needs stressing, the following stitches are useful: satin stitch (fig. 21); couching over one or more threads (fig. 76); zig-zag (figs 65 and 76); or cable stitch (fig. 76).

For more delicate work and a finer line, the straight stitch, either short or longer (figs 21 and 76) or whip stitch (fig. 76) will combine with satin stitch, etc.

Soft, merged effects are achieved not only by working over layers of transparent fabrics and nets, but by extending machine embroidered background stitchery over the edges of the applied shapes; figs 49 and 77 are striking examples of this treatment.

Many different background textures can be derived from stitches such as vermicelli and darning stitch (fig. 77) and can include working over small cut-out and applied pieces of velvet, felt, PVC, kid, cotton wool, organza, lace and bunched yarns of all kinds.

Enough has been suggested to show the infinite possibilities of combining machine and hand embroidery with appliqué; now it is for you to try out these ideas and to experiment for yourself. Examine the illustrations throughout this book, they should inspire you.

If machine-stitched appliqué is kept simple, it can be a quick way of producing a decorative effect (fig. 73), which makes it particularly suitable for dress decoration and for household linen. A fine machine-stitched line can be charmingly combined with applied shapes to make decorative patterns.

Freely and creatively machine-stitched appliqué is probably the speediest way to produce really large-scale projects, such as domestic and stage curtains, bedspreads, hangings, transparent window curtains and room-dividers, etc.

Fig 77 *Leopard* by Con Bolton (detail). Machine embroidery on screen-printed cotton

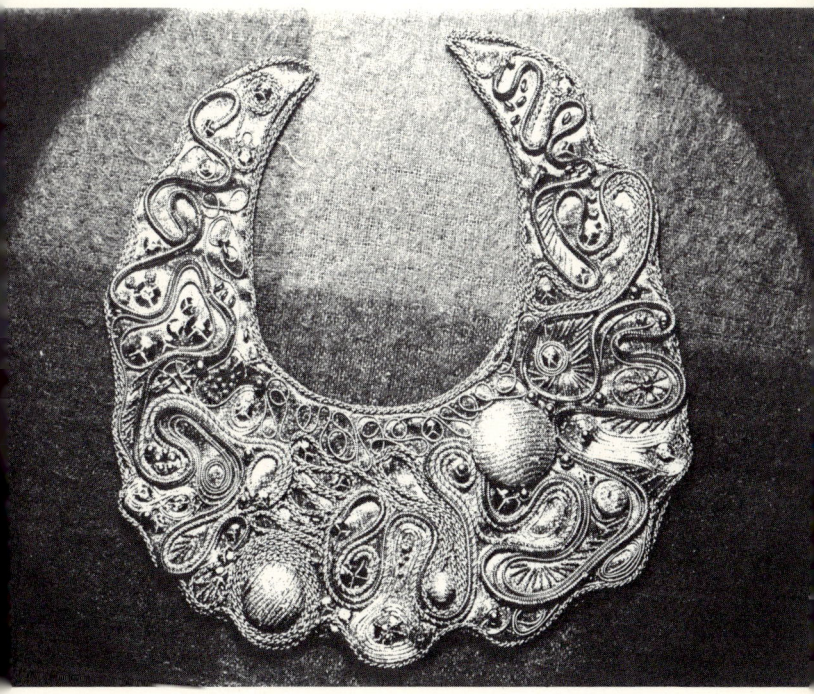

Fig 78  Combining gold-work methods with appliqué, Bucky King designed and made this golden collar

Over page
Fig 79  *Christ in Glory* designed and made by David Holt for Christ Church College chapel, Canterbury. 20 ft high in centre, 17 ft high at sides, 29 ft wide

Fig 80 Altar frontal, St Michael, Highgate. A good example, typical of early twentieth-century work; brow, green, orange and blue silks applied to cream silk

# 9 Appliqué for the church and theatre

Many people's reaction, when they think of appliqué in relation to the church, is to imagine dreary serge or shiny rayon brocades, with sentimental figurative subjects or meaningless foliated scroll patterns applied in satin and outlined with cords, the whole effect tending towards an illustration, and lacking all the subtlety and interest of embroidery today. This hardness is due, in part, to the practice of pasting the fabrics to combat puckering, thereby sacrificing the qualities of the fabric. This old-fashioned approach persists mainly because of the prejudice in favour of traditional conventions. (There are exceptions, which suit the surroundings; see fig. 80.)

Yet there is enormous scope for embroidered decoration, and especially appliqué, where a forward-looking attitude has been introduced and accepted, not only in the new churches but also in old cathedrals. Up-to-date appliqué can be integrated surprisingly well, and is a really viable proposition, adding colour and interest which will communicate in the idiom of today and therefore can be understood. And there is a real need for the work, and a sense of purpose in the undertaking.

The requirements for church vestments and furnishings vary from the permitting of book-markers, a cushion or pulpitfall to a full set of vestments for High Mass. Usually some form of decoration is acceptable and for this appliqué is very suitable for the following reasons:

1   Generally (but with the possible exception of the stole and scroll covers) vestments, banners, dossals, and soft furnishings are seen from a distance, therefore much finely stitched detail is lost, and so the broad colour effects obtainable when fabrics are applied are especially suitable (figs 81, 82, 83).

2   This naturally leads to the question of the scale of the design, because the decoration will have to 'tell-up', very probably, in some huge edifice such as a Gothic cathedral, so that large bold designs are preferable: and, as loosely woven backgrounds of textured fabrics can be used, so too, can exciting silks, velvets, metal fabrics, transparent nylons and nets be applied to obtain a slightly theatrical directness and impact. Well-known examples are the chasubles designed by Matisse for the chapel at Vence, France. (Reproductions can be obtained from the Museum of Modern Art, New York.)

There is now rather more latitude in the use of variations on the liturgical colours, and when including symbols within a design the approach is abstract and formalized rather than representational.

Fig 82 Chasuble by Marjorie Morton. Padded appliqué in blues and purple on lime green, with hand and machine embroidery

Fig 81 Chasuble for St Thomas in the Field, Gibsonia, Pa., USA, designed by Eliza Miller, executed by J. Phelps. Blue and white hand-woven silk

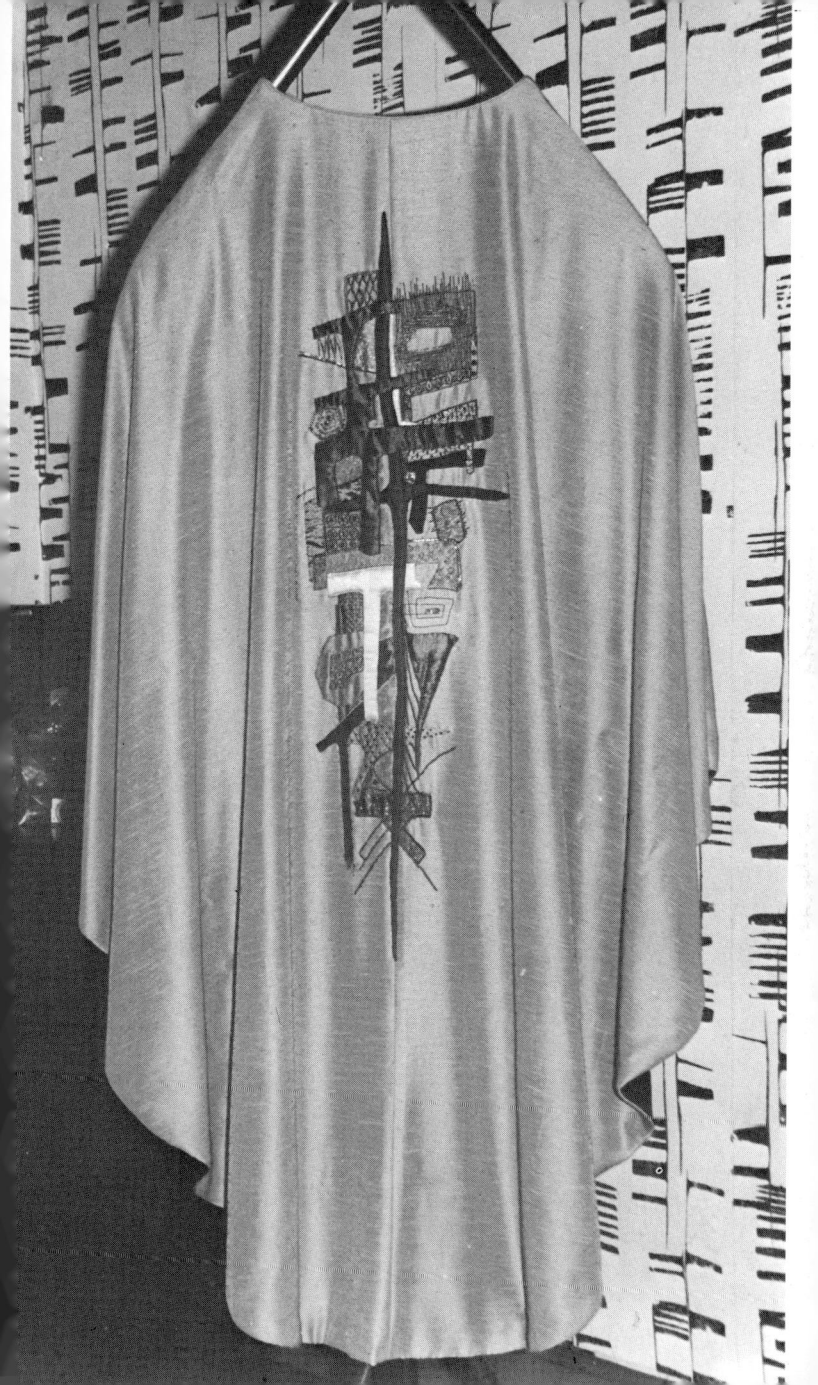

Fig 83 Chasubles by Olive Ferguson. Left, black moss crêpe with white felt and silver; right, red hand-woven silk with dark red Indian cotton applied

3 Apart from these aesthetic preferences for appliqué as a suitable technique for creating decorative effects, there are practical considerations: for example, the fairly general need for economy; and because this method is quicker to execute than is solid stitchery, it is less costly. Also, as ideas change so quickly now, it may even be an advantage for vestments, etc., to be expendable.

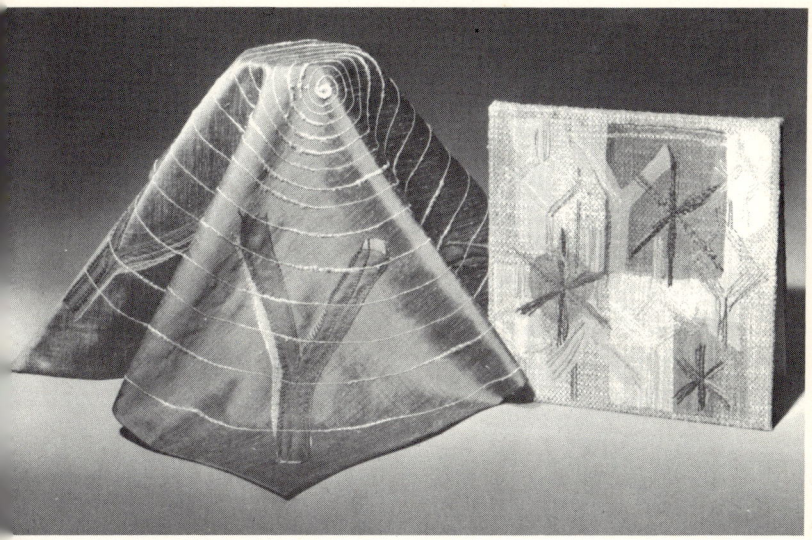

Fig 84  Burse and veil by Joan M. Gardner. Transparent fabrics applied to mustard yellow raw silk

We have seen that to undertake some forms of appliqué, previous experience is not necessary (though naturally it is an advantage in the manipulation of fabrics). By following the suggestions and instructions described for secular purposes, amateurs are perfectly capable of making their contribution by doing creative work for their churches. But it is advisable that all work of this kind should be guided by a trained instructor, and that when designing capabilities are weak a good designer who understands the demands of the craft should be commissioned to prepare something really original and not a re-hash from a traditional source.

This applies even more to group projects, for it is necessary that someone capable of seeing further ahead should plan the work. Because the capabilities of the individuals will vary, appliqué is the ideal technique to choose for carrying out a scheme. It gives pleasure to everyone taking part and skill quickly improves. This was found to be true by the members of a class for ecclesiastical embroidery who undertook to do a red cope, mitre, stole, five canon's copes, dalmatic and apparel for St Paul's

Fig 85 'St Peter', detail from red cope, a group project worked at Hammersmith College of Art and Building, for St Paul's Cathedral, London

Cathedral, London. The embroiderers embellished with couched metal threads the basis of appliquéd fabric, working in accordance with their individual ability but always keeping in mind the unity of the whole (fig. 85).

With careful planning, very large pieces such as hangings, curtains, altar frontals, etc., can be undertaken as co-operative works. Sometimes it is possible to divide up the area, either with the lines and shapes in the design, or with the seaming of the background, each width of fabric being worked separately, leaving overlapping pieces of the pattern to be sewn down after the joins have been completed. Although few amateurs have a large enough embroidery frame, when one is obtainable several people can work at the same time on one big piece of appliqué, such as an altar frontal.

Appliqué is unsurpassed in the creation of enormous textile hangings, because the artist can create in terms of great areas of coloured fabrics which can be judged as the work proceeds. For this, machine stitching is practicable, though it is difficult to manipulate so much material. It is essential to have a surface large enough on which to spread out the whole area when applying the pieces: when worked by hand with stitchery and threads, the scale, weight and bulk all present a problem. The great works by David Holt at Albuquerque (New Mexico) and the chapel screen of Christ Church College, Canterbury (U.K.) are two splendid examples (figs 79 and 88).

Whatever its size, work done for the church must be practical and made to withstand hard wear. On these grounds highly padded effects are sometimes criticized, but if strong fabrics, PVC or kid are used they will withstand the rub, and the advantages of the added dimension need not be sacrificed.

Much of what has been said above also holds good for theatrical work, but detail can be eliminated. Appliqué can be used in bold designs and colour schemes for proscenium curtains, or curtains for church or school halls, and for such things as cloaks, flags and banners. It is very suitable for group work in schools, where a needlework class could provide hangings or costumes for a school play, for example, or decorative hangings for the classroom. Even large scale work can be simply carried out by children with limited experience, under the supervision of the teacher.

For work to be seen close up on the television or cinema screen, where detail is important, embroidery and braids may be added to applied decoration.

Fig 86 (above) *Plastic Landscape* and (below) *From a concrete rubbing* by Margaret Hall

## 10 Finishing and mounting

Fig 87   Stretching the finished work

### Stretching

When appliqué has been carried out without the use of an embroidery frame it may be a little puckered. If so, pin it out, face downwards, upon an ironing blanket covered with a cloth; place another cloth over the back of the embroidery, and give it a good press; if necessary, use either a steam iron or a very slightly dampened cloth, though this is not always to be recommended.

If the work is badly puckered, then it will need to be thoroughly stretched. To do this you will need a board or other wooden surface large enough to take the embroidery. Cover this with a slightly dampened cloth or blotting paper; for a wool or linen background fabric it can be made damper. The board can be covered with polythene (polyethylene) first to prevent it absorbing the dampness.

With the right side of the embroidery uppermost, put the top left-hand corner to the corresponding corner of the board and hammer in a nail (drawing pins or thumbtacks can be used for small pieces of work). Pull out the longest side, parallel with the straight edge of the board, and put in another nail, then nail down along that edge at 1–2 in. intervals (fig. 87). Next, stretch out the opposite edge, parallel with that edge of the board; put in a nail at the corner, as before, and then pull the remaining corner into place so that all the corners form right angles, and again secure with a nail. Nail down this second long side, then the two shorter sides.

Allow it to dry out for twenty-four hours before removing.

Care should be taken with some silk fabrics as they may mark, especially if the damping is uneven.

## Mounting

For wall panels and any appliqué which needs firm, flat mounting, cut a piece of thin hardboard or strawboard (chipboard) to size, slightly smaller than the background fabric. If the work is to be framed, then allow an extra $\frac{1}{8}$ in. or $\frac{1}{4}$ in. all round, to allow for the edge to slip under the frame or decorative mount. Smooth down any rough edges, or cover the board with fabric. Mark the centre of each side. Put a tacked (basted) line round the embroidery to correspond with the edges of the board, and then mark the centre of this line on each side also.

With the appliqué face down on the table, put the covered board in position upon it. Match up the corresponding centre marks. First pin the centres of the top and bottom, turning the edges of the embroidery over and on to the board, then pin the centres of the sides. Next complete the pinning along the top and bottom, pulling slightly to tighten up the fabric. Repeat at the sides.

Using an ordinary needle, thread up a very long, strong thread and, starting from the centre and working outwards towards the corners, lace across the back, first from top to bottom, then horizontally. Mitre and stitch the corners, cutting away surplus fabric. (Instead of stitching, adhesive or sticky tape can be used; it is quicker, but not so satisfactory, as the tension cannot be adjusted so easily.)

Many embroideries are now finished in this way and attached to a covered mount, without a frame or glazing.

Altar frontals are usually mounted over wooden stretchers, for which the preparation is the same; but instead of lacing, fold the turnings over the stretcher, and secure by hammering in upholstery tacks, neatening with tape or unbleached calico.

For wall hangings and banners, use sail cloth, deck-chair canvas or dowlas (a coarse, half-bleached linen) etc., as an interlining, instead of a board. Cut this to the correct size and prepare as already described, but after folding the turnings of the embroidery over on to the back, herringbone or catch-stitch the edges to the interlining – but take care not to take the stitches right through.

For a banner, make up fabric loops (using interlining and lining), pin these in position along the wrong side of the top edge, and sew firmly in place (see fig. 10).

It is advisable to make tiny, invisible lock stitches at intervals of several inches around the outline of the embroidery, from the front of the work, to attach the fabric to the interlining. This is only necessary for very large pieces, and is difficult because of the stiffness of the interlining and because it must be done with the work laid out flat. A surgical needle helps.

To neaten the back, cut out a lining fabric to fit with an extra $\frac{1}{2}$ in. all round; pin it to the back, turn in the edges, slip stitch and lightly press this turning.

Fig 88 Detail of Reredos for the Church of Our Lady of the Assumption, Albuquerque, New Mexico. Designed and made by David Holt. The complete reredos consists of 117 panels 4 ft high × 3 ft wide, stretched on wooden frames, to cover an area of 1,600 square feet

# 11 Historical background

Fig 89 Detail showing King Mark and Tristram, with a squire in attendance. German, fourteenth century. Red, white, green and brown cotton and wool applied to dark blue woollen cloth, outlined with gilt leather strips. Victoria and Albert Museum

There has been little specific research on the subject of appliqué, and such a study might lead to the discovery of unknown examples from unexpected sources.

Undoubtedly there was a much earlier origin than extant pieces of applied work would suggest: in primitive civilizations and peasant cultures, unworn parts of discarded garments, etc., especially when made of silk, would have been cut into shapes and hemmed down, not only to repair but also to decorate other articles, from the sophisticated to the simple. Of this domestic work some of the earliest to survive comes from Germany. There is a fourteenth-century hanging, which shows Tristram and Iseult, now in the Victoria and Albert Museum, London (fig. 89). There are eleventh-century vestments in the Treasury of the Cathedral at Bamberg. Religious examples, being highly valued, were more likely to be preserved. Only a few isolated pieces of applied fabric can be found in English medieval church embroidery (mainly on chasubles of the early sixteenth century), apart from the custom of embroidering units separately on linen, cutting them out and sewing them to the velvet or silk background, with a cord or silk to neaten the edge and rays stitched in gold, and the addition of gold spangles to soften the effect.

It was for domestic and heraldic work that appliqué was so widely used in the Middle Ages; the fragments from the yellow, blue and white silk horse trappings of the third Earl of Albemarle (who died in 1260) are important, because, having been made into a seal bag, they were preserved, and are now in the British Museum. From the writings of Chaucer, and later from the Chronicles of Raphael Holinshed, we get some impression of the richness of the lavish embroidered decoration, much of which would have been carried out in appliqué for pennants, hangings, banners, surcoats, jupons (sleeveless surcoats worn over armour), and also for dress decoration. As a less costly substitute for solid embroidery, applied fabric has always been used.

During the Renaissance the woven brocades and damasks influenced the designs carried out in appliqué, which were usually of velvet and silk, the edges being outlined with cords, narrow leather throngs or couched silk. Although some of the Italian pilaster hangings were really a form of inlay, others were carried out in appliqué, as was much of the costume decoration. There are charming French and English examples of early seventeenth-century work based on plant form. Better known is the later Spanish work.

Of outstanding interest is the series of great allegorical hangings at Hardwick Hall, Derbyshire, made for the Countess of Shrewsbury in the late sixteenth century. They are twelve feet high and considerably wider. A typical subject, Faith, with a Turk reclining at her feet, is carried out in various fabrics applied to a background of black velvet (fig. 90). There are also many other panels; on some can be identified pieces of material from ecclesiastical vestments which, typically of the time, had passed into private hands at the Reformation. Impossible to convey is the experience of seeing all these incredible embroideries 'in situ' just as they

Fig 90 'Faith', with a Turk reclining at her feet. Hanging from Hardwick Hall, late sixteenth century. Victoria and Albert Museum

were left at the death of Bess of Hardwick in 1607. For detailed information M. A. Jourdain's 'English Secular Embroidery' should be consulted.

In Europe, during the sixteenth and seventeenth centuries, appliqué continued to be used for ecclesiastical work, also for secular furnishings such as bed valances and hangings, chair coverings, etc.; but when brocades and velvets became less costly, embroidered decoration declined.

The delicacy of rococo design rendered appliqué unsuitable as a technique; for this reason the panel shown in fig. 92 is unusual and interesting. Woollen materials have been applied to cream watered silk, parts remain unfinished and have been painted in watercolour. Details are worked in wools, silk and chenille. Many embroidery methods became fashionable in England during the eighteenth and nineteenth centuries, including the making of quilts, both pieced patchwork and appliqué.

Fig 91 Lectern cover. Italian, sixteenth century. Silk applied to velvet, outlined with cord

Fig 92 Panel, probably associated with a set of twelve designed by Robert Adam for insertion into the panelling of a drawing-room, c.1793

It was in the United States, where this art developed independently, that quilts reached such heights of perfection. The older examples were worn out through constant use, and only the later ones have survived, but the patterns were handed down from generation to generation. Thrift made the quilt popular in America (fig. 93); each scrap left over from cutting clothing was saved, and the women of the prairies turned to the worn out calicoes of their own dresses. The coldness of the winters made additional bedding essential, and the quilting-bee was a social factor. These gay, beautiful works are still prized possessions: there are several collections including those in the Brooklyn Museum, New York

Fig 93  Bridal quilt. American, mid nineteenth century. Plain and printed cotton fabrics, predominantly red and green, applied to white cotton ground, with part of the border padded. Smithsonian Institution, Washington, D.C.

City, in the Smithsonian Institution in Washington D.C., and in the Victoria and Albert Museum, in London. Although the resulting designs were so different, the method followed varied little: having decided which of the traditional designs would be used, the pattern was cut out in coloured fabric, allowing turnings, then this appliqué patch was basted to the foundation block, the edges were turned under and hemmed down. These blocks when completed were oversewn together, and the turnings pressed out flatly. The quilt back was then set in the frame and stretched, and the two layers of cotton filling were spread evenly. Over this was placed the appliquéd top: it was all tacked (basted) together, and

Fig 94  Woman's jacket. Hungarian, nineteenth century. Coloured leathers, mainly green, red and wine, applied to white. Victoria and Albert Museum

the whole area was quilted. From this simple basis all the variations of design have developed. Some of the designs were pictorial and the applied pieces were home-dyed. Occasionally, pieced patchwork was combined with appliquéd units; the whole was then quilted.

In Europe, during the nineteenth century, applied work continued more often as a peasant art: the Persian Resht (when not inlaid) possesses its own characteristics, being composed of felted woollen cloth, with strong outlines. There is the leather appliqué from Hungary: the woman's jacket shown in fig. 94 is an

Fig 95 Cushion cover. Scottish, about 1900. Green, blue and mauve silk, embroidered appliqué on linen. Victoria and Albert Museum

example, and there were also the shepherd's buckskin coats ornamented with applied coloured leather and stitchery, which were status symbols and often cost more than could be afforded.

Although William Morris had such a strong influence on design for embroidery, his daughter May seldom chose to carry out his designs in appliqué. However, others worked large pieces, such as portières, using this method. Rather later, appliqué featured prominently in the work of the Glasgow school, where the characteristic design had certain affinities to 'Art Nouveau'. Although the pioneering efforts of Jessie Newbery (fig. 95) and the teaching of Ann Macbeth belong to the Victorian era, the principles laid down for embroidery were much the same as those of today. By the 1930's the work and teaching of Rebecca Crompton was exerting its influence (fig. 96). She introduced the use of appliqué upon several layers of transparent gauze, and this elusive quality continues today stimulated by the wide choice of nylons and nets. Appliqué has now become very popular and is being developed in many interesting ways, as I hope this book has shown.

Fig 96 Appliqué by direct methods, by Rebecca Crompton, showing stitchery across the form, rather than the emphasis of outline. Cyclamen pink, scarlet and brown on cream

# For further reading

*Appliqué Stitchery* by Jean Ray Laury; Reinhold, New York, 1966
*Basic Design: the Dynamics of Visual Form* by Maurice de Sausmarez; Studio Vista, London and Reinhold, New York, 1964
*Creative Embroidery* by Christine Risley; Studio Vista, London and Watson-Guptill, New York, 1969
*Design in Fabric and Thread* by Aileen Murray; Studio Vista, London and Watson-Guptill, New York, 1969
*Embroidery Stitches* by Anne Butler; Praeger, New York, 1968
*English Secular Embroidery* by M. A. Jourdain (out of print)
*Ideas for Church Embroidery* by Beryl Dean; Batsford, London, 1968
*Ideas for Machine Embroidery* by Enid Mason; Mills and Boon, London, 1961
*Inspiration for Embroidery* by Constance Howard; Batsford, London and Branford, New York, 1967
*Introducing Machine Embroidery* by Ira Lillow; Batsford, London, 1967 and Watson-Guptill, New York, 1968
*Lettering for Embroidery* by Pat Russell; Batsford, London, 1970
*Pen Lettering* by Ann Camp; Dryad Press, London, 1964
*Simple Stitches* by Anne Butler; Batsford, London, 1968
*Stitchery, Art and Craft* by Nik Krevitsky; Reinhold, New York, 1966

# Index

Appliqué methods, basic 42 51
    blind 39, 42, 45, 59, 70, 71
    limited colour 57-9
    spontaneous 32-4
    using paper shapes 30, 36-42

Backing 16, 23, 25
Background 16, 23, 32, 33

Church, for use in 50, 59, 80-7
Colour, use of 14, 19, 39, 45, 57-9, 81
Couching 55, 57, 75
Curves, treatment of 41, 42

Design, ideas and sources 7-9, 19, 22
    preparation 9, 11, 37-9, 44-5
    transferring 28-31

Edges, treatment of 39, 42, 45, 55, 59, 75
Embroidery, machine 19, 34, 63, 71, 74-5
    surface 19, 34, 49, 50, 54-5
    see also 'Stitches'

Fabrics, background 16, 23
    choice of 16-19, 32-3
    transparent 19, 31, 39, 48, 59, 62
Felt 18, 55, 66
Frames 23, 58
    dressing of 23-6
Fraying 19, 33, 39, 47

Group projects 85, 87

Historical examples 94-101

Large projects 42, 51, 73, 87
Leather 55, 73, 87, 100

Lettering 64-5

Mounting 90-1

Padding 66, 67
Pellon 16, 39, 47, 64
Pouncing 28-9
Practical uses 57, 70-1
Puckering 16, 18, 43, 46, 75, 89
PVC 18, 55, 73, 87

Scale 19, 39, 81
Stayflex 16
Stitches, hand: backstitch 56
    buttonhole 63
    chain 56, 57
    Cretan 55, 56
    French knots 55, 56
    herringbone 55
    Pekinese 55, 56
    pin-stitching 59, 62
    running 49
    satin 54
    seeding 56
    slip-stitching 42, 63
    split 49
    stem 54
    straight 50
    trailing 63
    —machine 74-5
Stretching 89

Theatre, for use in 42, 87
Tone 14, 39, 44
Transferring 28-31

Vanishing muslin 75
Vestments 81-4, 85
Vilene 16, 39, 47, 64